Raising Kids Who Care

About Themselves,

About Their World,

About Each Other

Revised and Updated

KATHLEEN O'CONNELL CHESTO
Winner of the Emmaus Award

Foreword by Tom McGrath

Liguori
Lifespan

ONE LIGUORI DRIVE, LIGUORI, MO 63057-9999

Imprimi Potest:
Richard Thibodeau, C.Ss.R.
Provincial, Denver Province
The Redemptorists

ISBN 0-7648–1006-5
Library of Congress Catalog Number: 2002110866

Liguori Lifespan is an imprint of Liguori Publications.

An earlier edition of this book was originally published in 1996 by Sheed & Ward™.

To order, call 1-800-325-9521
www.liguori.org
www.catholicbooksonline.com

To Becky and Steve,
and all who work with
children at risk

Contents

Foreword

By Tom McGrath

Editorial Director for
TrueQuest Communications and
Prepare the Word
Homily Preparation Service

I remember, years ago, hearing the popular comedian Myron Cohen tell a story about a doting Jewish grandmother. She was walking down the beach with her precious grandson when a huge wave came up, drenching them both, and taking the boy out to sea. The grandmother fumed, and with one hand propped on her hip and the other shaking a fist toward the sky, shouted out, "God, he is mine own grandson. You return him to me immediately!"

At which point another huge wave came to shore and when it receded, there was the little boy, drenched but unharmed. The grandmother helped the boy to his feet, brushed off the seaweed, turned him around and inspected him from head to toe. All of a sudden she stopped, looked once again to the sky, and in that same loud voice, bellowed expectantly, "He had a hat!"

Like the woman in this story, Kathleen O'Connell Chesto

takes God seriously—seriously enough to stand toe-to-toe and cry out her fury to God's face. And, like the woman in the story, she cares ferociously about kids. She cares that way about her own kids (and now her precious granddaughter). And she cares about all children with that same fierce, unwavering love. She understands that parents do not want to deprive their children of what's best and what's rightfully theirs. And she knows that the greatest deprivation a child can endure is an underdeveloped spirit.

With passion, intelligence, humor, and grit (plus an enormous amount of sacrifice and plain hard work), she has had a fruitful career helping parents launch their children well into life, armed with the precious knowledge that they are more than consumers and that there's so much more to life than keeping ourselves amused; that they are, in fact, beloved children of God.

When, as a young mother, Chesto was first exposed to the Catholic teaching that parents are the first teachers of the faith, a strange thing happened. She took it seriously. Rather than letting this core teaching on family life drift by as a nice platitude, she ordered her life around it. With two small children at home and a third on the way, she returned to school to earn her Master's in Religious Studies. She says, "The whole purpose of getting my Master's degree was to make sure no one would stop me from doing my own religious education program with my family. Pretty much every step I took was influenced by my children."

She then had a revolutionary thought. Why not teach religion the way it has been handed down for centuries: with family and friends of all ages gathering and talking about their beliefs and their values; praying together, laughing together, learning together, being Church together? And why not do it in someone's home, to show our kids that God lives there, too? And so FIRE (Family-centered Intergenerational Religious Education) began, slowly at first, with hand-typed sheets handed out still damp from the mimeograph machine. The word spread—from parish to parish, from state to state, and around the globe. Chesto printed the first copies herself, paying for them by running a printing press for a local publisher.

And slowly, way too slowly, publishers began paying attention. Videos were made and sold. Books were written and published. Articles and interviews followed. Kathleen traveled far and wide as a much-in-demand parents'-night speaker, workshop presenter and eventually conference keynoter. Her message has always been the same: Awake to the God who loves you, who cares passionately about you, who calls you to abundant life.

For anyone who would ever try to make the case that family-based catechism somehow is too soft, too fuzzy, and ignores the core issues of faith, Chesto's own life provides a response. "Nothing in my life has had as much impact as having a family and having multiple sclerosis," she says. "My illness has shaped my spirituality. I feel like Jacob who struggled with the angel and asked for a blessing. He was left with a blessing and a limp. It fits!"

In the wake of the terrorist attacks of September 11, 2001, Chesto once again dares to stand toe-to-toe with God, asking, "Why?" She realizes that kids are asking "why?" too. And she knows that children deserve more than pre-fabricated answers that do not respect the depth of their questions. As Gregg Levoy wrote in *Callings*, "You don't want an answer you can put in a box and set on a shelf. You want a question that will become a chariot to carry you across the breadth of your life."

Through her teaching, her writing, and especially through the authentic person of faith she is, Kathleen O'Connell Chesto has inspired families to have the courage to engage such questions and to wait expectantly, like the grandmother on the beach, certain that God will indeed respond.

When I think of God as mother, Kathleen Chesto comes to mind. What I have come to know of this passionate woman speaks to me of a God who notices, a God who pays attention, a

God who aches to open our eyes to divine revelation unfolding before our very eyes in daily living and familiar relationships. Coming to know her has afforded me valuable clues about a God who, more than anything, yearns to give her children a vision of life that neither pain, nor sorrow, nor frailty, nor sickness, nor even death can overcome. That's the vision that illumines this book, and that shines on all who come to know her.

In the Wake of 9/11

Raising Kids Who Care was originally written when violence had a very different grip on us as a nation from what we have all experienced in the wake of 9/11. Violence in the nineties was seen as a more personal (or at least, national) problem: a problem in our schools and on our streets, in our families, our day-care centers, our homes for the elderly. We were focused on the children carrying guns to school, the juvenile homicide rate, the number of violent acts our children witnessed on television, the family violence statistics. Situations like Columbine and the copycat crimes that followed absorbed our entire attention as a nation.

We had almost stopped believing that violence on an international level could touch us. The cold war had ended, the Berlin Wall had come down, releasing the iron bands that had bound the earth's chest for forty years. We were no longer making movies like *The Day After* or *On the Beach*. It was almost as if we had convinced ourselves that the threat of a nuclear holocaust or third world war was over.

The truth of the world situation was something very different. Many smaller, more unstable nations had gained access to nuclear technology, India and Pakistan were testing nuclear bombs, the ongoing problems in Israel, Palestine, Ireland, and the new Russian satellite nations were growing increasingly volatile. While our own nation continued to make star wars technology a campaign platform, economic prosperity had turned the eyes of most average citizens inward. We may argue for the next ten years about what the FBI knew, didn't know, and should have known before the terrorist attack, but the simple truth is that most of us just weren't looking.

September 11 rocked our world. I walked the streets of New York, along with so many others, numb with grief, the ash that was not only buildings and paper but *people* clinging to our shoes and our clothing. I winced with each plane that flew overhead, too close, far too close. I looked into the eyes of the missing pasted on building walls, prayed at the impromptu shrines that had sprung up like wild flowers. And everywhere I heard New Yorkers greet one another with the never-ending questions: "Did you lose anyone?" "Where were you when the planes hit?"

It was the first time we had been attacked since Pearl Harbor. That attack, at least, was comprehensible; the world was at war. This time, we were attacked simply because of who we are. We were attacked in the name of God, a God reputed to hate us, reputed to call us the infidel. We were left with huge questions about just wars, about whether or not patriotism is the proper response to hatred, about a collective way to mourn our loss.

It has become difficult to talk about morality in the light of what happened and the way it happened. Too many times in the past year, I have heard explanations given to children about 9/11 that focused on what these "bad people" did. These were not bad people. That is part of what made the act such an atrocity. These were good people, religious people, fanatic people, willing to die for what they believed. They were not all that different from the people who gave us the Crusades.

As the realization that this attack was intentional began to sink in, one of the first things the news commentators told us was that there were only four terrorist groups in the world who were capable of such savagery. They were all religiously based.

The obvious conclusion to that finding is unsettling: Only religion could inspire such fanaticism.

Can we ever trust religion again? Can we ever again talk about a morality rooted in beliefs about God without clearly defining who that God is and what those beliefs are?

This little book was written before we faced these terrible questions. I was afraid that its simplicity might have no meaning for today's children and their parents, grown weary and wise in the face of terrorism. With some trepidation, I reread my own words in the light of what had happened. I was surprised to discover that this is *not* a book about religion at all. It is *not* about a church-inspired morality, but a book focused on a morality beyond the particularity of different faiths. This book looks at morality rooted in beliefs about what it means to be human.

There are some essential beliefs that belong to all of us. The laws we know as the Ten Commandments existed in similar form in ancient Sumerian culture and on Babylonian tablets long before they became part of the Hebrew Bible. Despite the commands of worship they contain, these are not religious laws. They are human laws. While they recognize an ultimate power beyond us, and are clear in our duty to worship, they place even greater importance on recognizing how to live with one another. (No cult, no religious teaching, should be allowed to take precedence over what our humanity tells us is true.) What made the events of 9/11 so horrendous for all of us is that they violated these human laws, and they were done in the name of God.

9/11 is as much an issue of personal morality as it is one of national security. A small sect allowed a certain leadership and its fundamentalist interpretation of the faith of an ancient religion to take precedence over their own moral compasses. We may hunt the perpetrators down in the hills of Afghanistan, we may bomb their hiding places and bring their leaders to trial, but we are still faced with the moral issue that allows a small group to believe that God could call them to kill thousands of innocent people. We will still all be haunted by the images of

Arab children dancing in the streets as the Twin Towers burned. We are faced with what happens when we lose touch with our humanity.

This book focuses on how that humanity develops. If no religion, no religious teacher or religious law, can take priority over what our conscience, our own inner voice tells us, then it is critical to attend to the development of that voice in each child, and to foster the courage and integrity necessary to follow it. Children in the wake of September 11, 2001, will have already begun their moral development by the time this book is in print; it really does start that young. While they will be totally un-aware of the tragedy that we have suffered, hopefully all of us will remain attentive to the wake-up call it has given us. We will need to be aware of the importance of providing an early and adequate setting for their moral compasses, of offering ample time and support as they practice being guided by them, of in-stilling in them the conviction that holiness is a matter of being truly human.

We still need to protect our nation against terrorism, to at-tend to the issues of injustice within our own boundaries, and to stand against terrorism and injustice in other nations. But the greatest hope for the future of the world is a deeply moral population. That morality can only be built one child at a time.

Introduction

It was the day before the final performance of the high school play when my daughter approached me: "No one else's parents will have the cast party."

I had offered the month before to host the cast party, but she had felt certain no one would want to come to the home of a freshman. She still did not feel too sure, and, since we had planned a dinner party for ten friends who were coming to see the play, I was not thrilled about the idea either.

After receiving her assurance that no more than ten or fifteen would show up, I threw a large tub of lasagna in the oven, ordered a cake, and prayed for good weather. Then I focused my attention on preparing for my own dinner guests. Nothing could have prepared me for the thirty-seven teenagers who descended upon our house that afternoon.

It was 5:30 p.m. when they arrived. Curtain call had been at noon and many had not eaten since breakfast, if they had eaten then. They approached the food table like a swarm of locusts. In a few moments they dispersed, leaving nothing behind them but a few paper plates. Any attempt to refill the table with whatever my husband or I could discover in the house produced the same swarming effect and the same stripped table. I had this tremendous urge to throw food to the ones who hung on the outside edges, much like you would feed the timid pigeons in the flock! The food demolished, attention turned to water fights. First water guns, then paper cups were employed in shattering the tension of weeks of rehearsal and three days of performances. In less time than it took to destroy the food, everyone was soaked. When the principal protagonists found a pail, I felt it was time to intervene. My choice of the moment was fatal. I stepped into a stream of water intended for a teen who ducked. Thoroughly sobered by this collision with reality, the teens turned to volleyball and dancing, while I returned, soaked, to my husband, who was valiantly attempting to entertain our dinner guests. Only one of our guests had children of her own, but all handled my divided and now soaked condition with a kind of humorous, loving endurance.

As the sun disappeared, we handed out dry shirts and collected wet clothes for the dryer. A few dedicated souls returned home to do homework, but the majority squeezed into our very small family room to watch a suspense movie. Shrieks and squeals floated up the stairs to the intimate group of adults I had finally managed to join in the living room. When I forced myself to break away and headed down the stairs with dry clothes, I found bodies on every available inch of space: the couch, the back of the couch, the tables. Across the length of the floor, fifteen bodies were lying sideways, so tightly packed that no one could move without the whole group getting up!

Our dinner guests were gone long before my daughter's friends dragged upstairs to use the phone or to head out to their cars. When the last one left, Liz curled up on the couch next to me.

"I had a great time, Mom."

Hardly an earth-shattering revelation or an ardent avowal of devotion, but I knew it meant, "I love you." My husband and I dragged ourselves to bed chuckling over our own haphazard dinner party, knowing our friends had probably gone home silently affirming their own choice to remain childless, but also appreciating the need for the teens to be given priority on this particular occasion.

There are few times or places left in our society that teach the value of putting others first. Ours is a self-centered, me-first generation, and this is the society into which today's children are born and indoctrinated. There are a few, scattered examples of heroic selflessness, like Mother Teresa and Archbishop Romero, but the ordinary, everyday kind of unselfishness has been forgotten. Spirituality itself has become a type of exercise in self-improvement, a "me and my relationship with God" operation.

The concept of family stands in stark contrast to this message. Family proclaims that the basic reality of existence is communal. It reflects in ordinary, unassuming ways what Roman Catholicism has always taught in liturgical ways: a relationship with God exists only as part of a relationship with others. "How can I love a God whom I cannot see, if I don't love my brother or sister whom I can see?"

Family is where we acquire the ability to see another's need at a given moment as greater than our own. It can be as simple as allowing the person who has to leave the house first to get into the bathroom first. It can be as traumatic as choosing to open an intimate dinner party to thirty-seven boisterous teens. No one ever called it holiness or spirituality. We were simply taught to think of it as sharing.

Affluence is placing a great strain on our ability as families to teach self-sacrifice. When Jesus spoke about how difficult it would be for the rich to enter heaven, it had to have something to do with our inability to learn sacrifice in a situation of plenty. Sharing works best when there is not enough, from not enough money for new clothes to not enough lasagna or floor space for a cast party. A television for every room, individual phones and separate lines may eliminate arguments, but they also inhibit community and the possibility of learning to live with and for others. If there are fewer arguments in our families today, it could be because there is less conversation. If we are not careful, affluence could deprive us of some of our greatest family values.

Time is the only commodity that seems to be rapidly decreasing as material things increase in our lives. Society teaches that time is money, and the mindset often overflows into family life. We guard our time with miserly concern, preach endlessly to our children about using time constructively and spending it wisely, and we complain continuously about all the things that take time. Living in a family requires that we surrender time to one another. First steps, first words, impromptu picnics, and teenage confidences are not subject to schedule, but they cannot "take" our time if we choose to give it freely. It only requires a simple change in how we look at things. It no longer "takes time" to give a child a ride, tell a story, or listen attentively; we have decided to give this child the gift of ourselves at this particular moment. Aquinas calls this spirituality the "sacrament of the present moment." Families call it being available.

If we are going to make a difference in the lives of the children in our families and in our classrooms, that difference will begin with being available. Just as young children rely on us to provide for their physical needs, they are also dependent on us for the emotional and psychological support that will enable them to grow into ethical, caring adults.

This book is based on the assumption that you choose to be available to them, that you have decided that our children and our families are worth our effort. It is a compilation of essays that initially appeared as a column under the title "Helping Today's Children." They have been rewritten for this context. The original column explored the spiritual and moral development of children and the particular problems they face growing up in today's world. The suggestions and insights of those columns are offered here for those who believe we are capable of making a difference, that family values are more than a tool for politicians seeking office, and that it is possible to create a more loving, less violent society for the next generation.

My daughter returned home from school the day after the party, still glowing. "It was awesome, Mom. Everyone said so. A cast party that will go down in history."

The day *had* been awesome. It held within it a deep understanding of what it means to be family, of the satisfaction and pleasure that can be found in placing the needs of someone you love before your own, of the fun that can be had in the simple enjoyment of one another's presence, even when food and space are at a minimum. These are the real family values. This is the message society is failing to teach. If we fail to teach it as family, we run the risk of allowing our world to lose its soul.

Most of our efforts will not go down in history. But the sacrifices we make and the lessons we teach will remain etched deeply in the hearts of the children whose lives have collided and become intertwined with ours.

PART I

Growing Morality

OUR SON CRAWLED ACROSS THE *NEW YORK TIMES* spread out on the living room floor. As he crawled, he pointed and named the capital letters in the headlines. Two letters caught his attention and he read them repeatedly, T…V, T, V, TV." A light dawned slowly on his face. He scooted to the television, pointed at the screen and said triumphantly, "TV!" We watched in amazement as we realized that our one-year-old son, who still could not walk, was reading. He went from letters to words to sentences to books with a rapidity that frightened us, as he entered a love affair with the written word that eventually took him into graduate school in journalism. He did not walk until he was fifteen months old.

Our second child walked early, danced and jumped almost as soon as she walked, and struggled with reading. The concepts were too abstract; she would learn a word only to forget it the next time it appeared on the page. When she was seven, I spent a summer teaching her to cook from a children's cookbook, giving concrete form to the abstract words, and eventually watched the same miracle of recognition dawn in her eyes. She, too, jumped quickly from words to sentences to stories; she, too, learned to love reading for its own sake. Today she is happiest when she is curled up in a corner with a good book.

Physical and intellectual development follow fairly predictable patterns in young children, but children may bring very different natural abilities to it, abilities which often affect the timing of that development. The same is true for moral development. Sociologists of the last decades have determined that morality begins in empathy. As parents, we have all witnessed that natural empathy children have for those who are hurting. As parents, we have also been aware, perhaps only on a subconscious level, of the different ages at which this empathy is manifested. We have seen the two-year-old who attempts to respond to another's tears with caresses or a favorite toy, and we have witnessed the two-year-old who ignores or hides from the other's pain. Children appear to be born with varying degrees of empathy that develop at different rates, in a manner similar to their physical and intellectual evolution. How that empathy develops into moral reasoning and what we as parents and teachers can do to enhance that development is the focus of Part I of this book.

CHAPTER 1

Do Feelings Count?

During the second week of October, our nation observes "Character Counts" week, a bipartisan effort of a beleaguered Congress to restore value education to our schools. Throughout the 1980s and 90s, when teen violent crime rose 700 percent, when the rate of teen pregnancy rose alarmingly along with the rate of sexually transmitted diseases, when the number of homicides committed by children went up some 400 percent, where children were deprived of a good education because so much of the effort of the schools was directed toward maintaining discipline and order, and where children became victims of drugs and violence at a frightening rate, people turned in desperation to politics for the answer.

But if the increasing crime, sex, and violence resulted in uniting the traditionalists, conservatives, and many of the liberals on the need for ethical values, there is still no agreement on what those values are, who should decide what we teach the children, when it should be taught, or what is the best way to teach it. Many of our political figures are still too busy with the "blame game" of deciding who is responsible for the lack of values in our children to offer constructive help in laying a better ethical foundation for our society. If we hope to achieve any lasting changes, they will need to be built on a better understanding of morality, how it can be fostered in the family, and what are the aspects of today's society that offer the most critical challenges.

Social science in the last twenty years has made enormous strides in understanding our concept of morality and its development in children, but those findings have been consistently overlooked in both the political sphere and in the Church. The Church has long held that morality is cognitive, inextricably bound up with reaching the "age of reason." Morality has been understood as the ability to "know" right from wrong, a level of understanding commonly designated as age seven.

Yet very early sociological studies done with elementary school children demonstrated that the knowledge of a moral code of adults (such as the Ten Commandments or Scout Oath) had little to do with the moral behavior of the children involved.[1] Repeated studies have left very little doubt that a child's shaky memory and sketchy internalization of such rules has limited implication for the child's tendency to be honest, kind, or obedient. At the same time, it is obvious that children do have a moral sense, a sense that appears to develop independently of adult codes and long before the mythical "age of reason."

The four-year-old who pleads, "That's not fair," often has as strong a sense of injustice as the adult whose rights have been violated. The three-year-old is capable of sharing and feeling intense guilt or real sorrow over another's pain. Very young children often know how to play fair, be kind, and remain loyal. Today, most sociologists agree that these moral actions in children are rooted in "moral feelings" rather than in cognitive decisions.[2]

Feelings such as empathy, sympathy, admiration, shame, anger, and guilt are the various threads that make up the

[1] H. Harthstone and M. A. May, *Studies in the Nature of Character.* New York: Macmillan, 1928, 1930.

[2] Jerome Kagan, *The Nature of the Child.* New York: Basic Books, 1984.

tapestry of our moral reactions to human situations. These feelings are frequently stronger incentives, even for adults, to act in accordance with our moral standards than the standards themselves. It is these moral emotions, acted upon, affirmed, and supported, that eventually lead to the development of a moral value system.[3]

The first moral feeling identified—and the one most basic to all morality—is empathy. The ability to feel another's pain, pleasure, distress, or need is the foundation of virtue. We may cognitively acknowledge another's pain, as we do every time we read the newspaper, but unless we "feel" that distress, we will probably not be moved to act upon our knowledge.

Empathy is a universal human trait. Infants in a nursery will respond to the cry of another infant. Babies as young as nine months will be disturbed by another child's anguish and will make efforts to comfort. The attempt to help begins as self-centered; children offer what they themselves need in that situation.

When my youngest was not quite two, I fainted on the kitchen floor. When I came to, she had covered me with her blanket and placed her favorite stuffed animal by my head. Her eyes were red and she had obviously been crying only moments earlier, but she had set aside her own fear in order to "help." She had offered the only support she knew, and her choice demonstrated the ability to put another's need first, empathy becoming compassion.

Children show varying degrees of empathy, even at birth. Crucial to the growth of this emotion is the development of imagination. The child must be able to understand how the other feels and must be socialized to take those feelings seriously. Games of make-believe are exercises in empathy that give a child the opportunity to try on another's role, its frustrations and its

---

[3] William Damon, *The Moral Child.* New York: Free Press, 1988.

pleasures. Stories that offer a child the opportunity to identify with the people or animals that inhabit them enhance the beginnings of empathy. Scripture stories and many of the children's classics offer role models for virtue. Videos and family television shows that tell tales of virtue and courage can be helpful if they are discussed in the family and related to events in the family's own life. It is the ability to empathize with the characters in the stories, to choose them as heroes worthy of emulation and imitation, that can enhance the development of virtue in the life of a child.

As parents, our recognition of the importance of empathy has been instinctual. We may have given lip service to the idea of an "age of reason" as we accepted Church explanations regarding proper ages for sacraments, but in teaching our children foundational ethics, we relied on empathy. None of us believed that our children had to be six or seven years old to understand that stealing was wrong, but we did not base that belief on a commandment, no matter how strongly we ourselves might have understood it to be the basis of our actions. We simply asked our children, "How would you feel if someone took *your* crayons?" Our own instincts tell us that the ability to feel what the other is feeling is far more important in making a moral decision than knowing an external code.

Empathy is fostered by relationships. Wherever human beings gather to plan, work, or play, rules of conduct, feelings of care, and a sense of obligation follow in varying degrees. Since children are involved in relationships almost from birth, it is inevitable that moral thoughts and feelings will arise. Learning to understand and appreciate the needs of the other and of the group—and to treat those needs with respect—mark not only the growth of empathy, but the development of morality in the child. But this growth does not happen automatically and is frequently short-circuited in those young lives with few meaningful relationships.

In a 1992 study on teen violent crime in the United States,

the most frightening finding was not the high rate of violent crime among teenagers, but the total lack of empathy or feelings of responsibility that most young criminals had for their victims. A fifteen-year-old in New York City walked onto a train and shot eleven people, not because he was angry or hurting, but because he was bored. A group of preteen boys tortured and beat a young pony to death, and were still laughing about it when the police arrived. A sixteen-year-old on death row explains that he walked into a convenience store and shot two people because it seemed like a good day for someone to die. The crimes, as terrible as they are, are not what horrify us. It is the total lack of caring, the absence of an empathy we have come to view as an essential part of being human, that makes these teenage crimes and criminals so abhorrent to us. In one teen detention center in New Hampshire, a group process was designed to help teen offenders develop a sense of empathy by forming relationships within the group and inviting the group to reflect on relationships with victims. The message is clear by default. If we want to raise ethical children, we must pay careful attention to the development of empathy.

Since empathy begins in relationship and imagination, we must seek ways to foster these realities with infants and young children. We belong to a culture that is forgetting the importance of relating. We seldom eat meals together, and when we do, the television distracts us from the awesome task of communicating. Our outdoor recreation involves watching others compete, perhaps our own children, but not actually playing together. Our indoor recreation has become even more passive and isolated, our main interactions happening with video screens and computers, involving little or no imagination or empathy. At one time, we built porches on the fronts of our houses, where we would sit together in the evenings, on swings and rockers, and chat with the neighbors. Today, we build decks on the back of our houses to offer privacy and isolation.

We can do without the front porches and their swings, but

we cannot survive without the conversation and companionship they fostered. Television and team sports have their place, but not in place of mealtime conversation and family stories and games. Empathy develops slowly and requires huge investments of time on the part of parents and teachers, particularly in the early stages. But if we hope to raise ethical children, we simply cannot be too busy to spend time reading, playing, talking, and dreaming with them. Moral education cannot be allowed to become a political tool, a catch phrase or platform for an election year or a particular party. It is the educational right and developmental need of every child and the "moral" duty of every parent and teacher.

For Parents

1. Visit your local library, and ask for a list of age-appropriate stories that teach strong values. Read the stories out loud. Ask children how they would feel if they were the principal character in a story. How would they have acted? When events come up in the children's own lives, ask them how they think the storybook character might have handled a particular situation.
2. Teach children to evaluate their actions by using "how would you feel…" questions.
3. Have family meals. If having one every day is impossible, aim for at least three a week. Turn off the television, and talk to each other.
4. If you have not read *Fahrenheit 451* by Ray Bradbury, read it and share it with your teenagers.

For Teachers

1. Make an open-ended story part of every lesson. Allow the children to discuss the ways they think it should end, and invite them to share it with their parents.
2. Foster discussions on feelings in the classroom.

CHAPTER 2

Aren't You Ashamed
of Yourself?

She was twelve years old, blonde, blue-eyed, with the innocent face of an angel. And she was lying through her
teeth. When I confronted her with that fact, she smiled sweetly
and said she must have been mistaken. There was something
incredibly upsetting in her response—something missing from
her reaction to being caught—that unnerved me. Her answer
had been completely neutral, as if there was simply no difference between the truth and a lie, and I realized on reflection
that what had upset me so acutely was the total absence of shame.

Shame is one of the earthy emotions that has been labeled
as basically neurotic anxiety. It is the feeling of embarrassment
one has in failing to act in accordance with perceived behav-
ioral standards. Much of psychology has held, since Sigmund
Freud, that the capacity for shame is induced in early childhood
by confrontations between toddler and parent, particularly
around the issue of toilet training. The child reacts with embarrassment to failures, and feels humiliated when a parent shows
displeasure or disgust. As the child incorporates the parent's at-
titudes toward the failure into his or her psyche, the child becomes "ashamed."

It is these possible unpleasant inner consequences for the child that have given both shame and guilt their bad reputations. Erik Erikson places shame in opposition to autonomy, and guilt in opposition to the development of initiative. Erikson argues that shame and doubt, which first appear in "toddlerhood," are the natural enemies of self-control and threaten children's ability to stand on their own and move on to the next stage of development. Shame turned in on the self is, in fact, a very destructive emotion. But actions that induce shame and the emotion they elicit do not necessarily have to destroy our sense of self.

Today, psychologists argue that shame has an important place in the development of morality. Children can be taught at a very early stage to recognize that a particular action is shameful because it is not what is expected of them, without seeing themselves as shameful people. Trust is first internalized when children recognize that the significant adults in their lives expect certain behaviors of them and that they are capable of fulfilling them. Shame is the result of failing to live up to that trust; trustworthiness is the result of repeated successes.

Since trustworthiness is the goal, success is important. It is vital that parents' expectations are reasonable and represent things over which the child is capable of exercising control. Children are capable of obeying simple directives, like "Don't touch" and "Put your toys away," long before they have mastered the complexities of bladder and bowel control. Using humiliation as a punishment, or "shaming" a child by insinuating that she is not capable of living up to the trust placed in her, will induce a destructive form of shame, the shame that is the basis of Erikson's dichotomy. But it is important to realize that internalized trust, a self-esteem that enables a child to see herself as a trustworthy person, will also bring a sense of shame at failure. This shame can be a powerful deterrent in learning to avoid actions that the significant adults in a child's life have labeled as evil.

Guilt appears later in childhood than shame, and is not as dependent on the parent/child relationship. Like shame, it is the awareness that we have failed to live up to a particular standard. In guilt, however, it is not the embarrassment at being found out but the failure itself that stimulates the emotion. We are capable of feeling guilt for our actions or our failure to act even when those actions are known to no one but ourselves. Most of us grew up referring to this internalized sense of right and wrong as "conscience."

Like shame, guilt can be neurotic or healthy. With empathy, a child feels discomfort over the distress of another, but guilt allows the child to further recognize in what way he or she may be responsible for the other's discomfort. Guilt first appears around the age of two with the simple awareness of causing another pain. Healthy guilt later becomes more complex as the child recognizes the failure to attempt to relieve the distress of the other, even if he or she did not cause it. By the age of three, a child begins to be aware of hurting not just another's body or possessions, but hurting another's feelings. A mature sense of guilt, seen in children as young as ten, eventually develops into the capacity for self-criticism in order to develop a better relationship with others.

Teaching children to internalize trust depends on being able to recognize and support feelings of shame and guilt without manipulating them to achieve subservient behavior. How we welcome a child back who has been excluded for misbehavior will have a great impact on the child's ability to internalize the rule as something that is for the good of the whole. We need to take a moment to let our children know we forgive them and we still trust them, we miss their presence when they misbehave, and we know they want to behave better in the future. This affirms their own belief in their ability to be trustworthy, while acknowledging the shame of failure.

It is important to focus on how the behavior makes the individual child feel, and how his or her behavior affects the others in a group, rather than on how it makes us, parent or caregiver, feel. We want children to be able to do something because it is the right thing to do, it makes them feel good about themselves and often makes their peers feel good about them. This allows their natural empathy to inform a sense of true guilt. We do not want the basic learning to be that a rule is something that must be obeyed because there is someone bigger around to enforce it.

When a child has made a serious mistake, it is important to discuss the consequences and help the child to consider some possible remedies or solutions. The goal is to foster autonomy in the child by offering ways to correct the wrong at the same time we are reinforcing the child's sense of responsibility for having caused the problem. If a child is to develop a healthy sense of guilt for wrongdoing, he or she needs to be free to make mistakes and try again. Forgiveness becomes crucial at this point in a child's moral development. If we continually bring up past failings, we have not forgiven, and the child will find it difficult to forgive herself. Forgiveness does not mean that we are relieving the child of taking responsibility for an action. Forgiveness implies that we expect the child to take full responsibility, so it is no longer necessary for us to harp on the failure.

Guilt and shame help us to recognize that a given action is evil. As such, they are uncomfortable emotions that prod us to a higher standard of behavior, a standard set for us by someone who believes in us. Forgiveness teaches us that we are trustworthy people, capable of taking responsibility for our mistakes, even when assuming that responsibility is painful. If we want to protect our children from ever feeling bad about anything, we may be depriving them of emotional skills they need to grow into moral people in our society.

For Parents

1. Talk with children about feelings of shame and guilt. Help them to begin to understand the role of these emotions in promoting good behavior. Share with them some of your own feelings of shame and guilt. It is important for children to recognize that these feelings remain with us for a lifetime, and that we consider them guides in our decision-making.
2. Children of seven or eight years of age are old enough to be interested in the fact that different actions cause shame in different cultures. Ask your librarian for help in discovering stories that deal with issues of honor in Native American and Asian cultures.
3. Talk with children about forgiveness, the things you personally find hard to forgive, and why.

For Teachers

1. Read the stories of Peter and Judas in the Passion narratives. Talk with students about the shame and guilt both of them were feeling. Why did they react so differently?
2. Tell the story of Joseph and his brothers. How did the shame and guilt of Judah help him to behave differently toward Benjamin than he had toward Joseph?

CHAPTER 3

A Scaffold for Justice

S he was a newcomer at noon to the girl's side of the playground. Although she had been with us since first grade,
her mother drove her home every day for the long lunch hour.
She had the rare distinction in our small, country school of being an only child, and today, she had a long jump rope.

Assuming that such a rope was meant to be shared, I suggested, "Let's play run through the boiler." My suggestion was
greeted with a small chorus of "No ends," and the two unlucky
girls who had joined us last reached for the rope.

We were astonished when Debbie screamed, "It's mine!" and
wrapped the rope several times around each hand, and then
jumped off sullenly. We stood stunned for a moment until someone shouted "Red Rover, Captain Uphill!" It was the coveted
position for the game, but I quickly recovered with "Captain
Downhill!" and we began to choose sides, distributing the smaller
children evenly, and heading for the hill that was always the site
of the game.

We were losing (the downhill team always lost) when Debbie
wandered over to the game. "I choose Debbie," I shouted, before anyone else had noticed her. She may have been stingy, but
she was still one of the fastest runners in the school, and we
needed all the help we could get. She slipped into the position I

assigned her, leaving her jump rope on the ground behind her. She never brought it to school again.

There is no better example of children's morality than sharing. Sharing is a normal part of the life of every child, beginning as soon as the child interacts with others. Children will share spontaneously in early childhood as a way to entice others to play with them or as entrance into a desired group. They discover, often by chance, that joint play is frequently more enjoyable than solitary play, and the enjoyment becomes its own reason for sharing. They will share to protect themselves from exclusion or anger on the part of another child. Sharing itself can become a playful ritual, the process of turn-taking as important and as much fun as the game itself. While the reasons for sharing may be less than noble, as my own childhood memory attests, the formative value of the repeated action outweighs all other considerations.

Empathy offers a compelling motive for a more unselfish form of sharing. Parents naturally invoke the feelings of others when encouraging children to share (e.g., "Mary will be sad if you don't share your ice cream"), and this kind of reasoned urging promotes a norm of kindness that supports a child's natural feelings of empathy. While the child may give in simply because an authority figure gently insists on sharing, it doesn't lessen the importance of fostering empathy as the primary driving force for the action. Drawing a child's attention to the pleasure she has given another by sharing ("Look how happy you made Mary") builds on the child's feelings of empathy. Consistent, reasoned, adult encouragement of the child's natural empathy for others is necessary to the development of a firm sense of obligation to share. Even when children choose not to act on this obligation, there will be an internal belief in sharing as a necessary part of any social relationship, and that this is "right" and a failure to share is "wrong."

Sharing becomes the basis for a child's first formulations about what is "fair." "Fair," to the primary school child, means identical or "equal" parts for each person. "Fair" expands in the first three years of school to include the concept of merit, "those who work harder, or are more talented, get more." Eventually, a fully developed sense of justice will include the concept of benevolence, the granting of special consideration to those whose need is greatest.

The complex systems of judgment and action that develop in the process of learning to share are the foundation of moral decision making. We live in a society that often short-circuits the development of a true sense of justice, never actually reaching "benevolence," simply presenting merit as the only true measure of "fairness." We cry out against the parable of the laborers in the vineyard who worked the whole day and were paid no more than those who worked the last hour. We believe the only equity is the one that gives the most to those who work the longest, without considering the equality of opportunity, education, or need. Children of affluence, who frequently have little reason to share within their homes, are being offered excuses by a neoconservative society for not sharing outside their homes and communities. Real sharing represents the ability to consider not just the rights but the feelings and needs of others; real sharing recognizes the need of the other as a "right." Real sharing is the child's introduction to the Gospel's fundamental option for the poor.

Most of the world's great battles have been fought by those who were contending for their "fair share." Many of those battles began on the playground. Consistent generosity, whenever and wherever it exists, is the result of long-term moral development.

For Parents

1. Provide opportunities for sharing. Rather than praising children for sharing, focus their attention on the pleasure they have given to another by their actions.
2. Be a model of generosity for your children. Enlist their help in bringing food to the food bank, clothing for the clothing drives. Share your home and your possessions with others openly.
3. We cannot prevent a child from being hurt by one who refuses to share. Comfort them in their pain, and take time to point out just how much not sharing hurts. Encourage them to treat the offender with kindness.

For Teachers

1. Read the parable of the laborers in the vineyard. Invite the children to discuss the behavior of the owner. Why does God sometimes act in ways that seem unfair to us?
2. Read the parable of the talents. What does it say about sharing?
3. Invite your class to discuss moments in their lives when it is particularly hard to share.

CHAPTER 4

Family Rules and
Moral Citizens

There is a long-standing rule in our home that whoever prepares the meal does not have to participate in cleanup. As the children grew up and left for college, the rule became less necessary as meal preparation became simpler and cleanup faster. But every time they returned for the holidays or semester break, and everyone's favorite dish found its way to the table, each of our budding cooks was grateful for the rule. That is the wonderful thing about rules: They develop a life of their own that is separate from all our explanations and enforcement. They eventually become part and parcel of what children have internalized as "just," and no longer require parental force or penalties (although a little nagging is sometimes in order).

All societies delegate authority, and these delegations must be respected and obeyed if a society is to survive. The basic understanding of this delegation and the respect for authority which it assumes begin in family rules and the manner in which they are taught. Legitimate authority serves the interests of both the subordinate and leader. When that type of authority is modeled and taught from toddlerhood through teen years, there is a strong possibility of producing moral citizens who are equally capable of respecting just laws and challenging unjust ones. If we accept this as a basic premise, then the high rate of teen crime and amoral behavior is rooted not only in the presence of guns and violent media, but in the absence of family rules and supportive family structures.

A rule is a regulation that governs conduct within a certain society. When family rules overlap with society's rules, such as prohibitions against dishonesty and violence, children learn the double message that this is not only wrong here, it is wrong in society at large. For this reason, the parent (or principal nurturer) has a critical and irreplaceable role in the moral development of the child. It is the parent's responsibility to inform a child of the rules within the family and beyond it, to enforce the sanctions, and to communicate to the child their social purpose. The manner and the consistency with which the primary caregiver explains and insists upon compliance in the first two years of life has great bearing on the later moral or not-so-moral behavior of the child. A child's respect for authority is the single most important moral legacy from the parent/child relationship.

Sociologists recognize three basic patterns of rule enforcement in the family (and later in the classroom). Power assertion uses the superior physical strength or authority of the parent or teacher to force the child to conform. It is most effective in the short term, and frequently needs to be used in situations where a child is in danger. It is reasonable to slap the hand of a toddler who reaches for a hot pan, to physically remove a child who is behaving roughly on a gym set, to put a child who is having a temper tantrum in a room and close the door. Power assertion addresses the immediate problem, but it does nothing to effect the long term internalization of a rule. A child is more apt to remember the pain inflicted than the rule violated, and will behave in the prescribed manner as long as someone bigger is there to enforce the rule. Too great a show of force actually encourages children to attempt to do the forbidden thing when no one is watching.

Power assertion can have other negative side effects. It is capable of teaching children that force is the way to get someone smaller to do what you want. Most parents would be shocked to discover how much the use of power assertion resembles bullying in the eyes of the child.

Love withdrawal as punishment has longer lasting effects, but does little to develop independent moral behavior. Because most of us want to believe our children love us enough to comply with our requests, it is easy to interpret misbehavior as a lack of love, or to use a child's love to manipulate obedience. However, when a child is taught to behave simply out of love for parents, the child's actions become dependent on the parental belief in what is right and wrong and on the need for parental approval. Standards of behavior remain dependent on an external criterion, on the presence or absence of an authority figure to approve or punish, rather than the child's own internal sense of right and wrong. Love withdrawal is capable of inducing both lying and cheating on the part of the child who fears losing a parent's approval.

"Inductive" is the name sociologists give to a pattern of rule enforcement that offers the best possibility of producing independently ethical children. In inductive rule enforcement, the child's compliance with the rule is ensured through some minimum form of control. At the same time, the child is told the reasons behind the standards and the consequences of unacceptable behavior. Children need to be prevented from certain actions, but they also need to know why those actions are disruptive and how they hurt others. This method of rule enforcement often takes the form of questioning the child and allowing space for the child to acknowledge and take responsibility for the rule.

"Is that where your shoes belong? Someone could trip if you leave them there." The goal of induction is to provide enough force for the child to act properly, and enough explanation through persuasion and reasoning for the child to come away from the encounter with an understanding of why the rule is important.

Firm parental control, mixed with responsiveness, clear communication, and understanding of the maturity level of the child involved, has been shown to foster a sense of social responsibility and competence in the young child. Children from homes where rules are enforced in this manner exhibit not only respect for adult laws, but the ability to cooperate with peers in constructing rules to govern childhood playing and sharing.

A system of family rules, rules about bedtime, household responsibilities, television viewing, company, involvement in activities, a system of rules that have been reasonably clarified in the applicable situation, simplifies family life since each request or action does not require its own separate decision. Family rules offer children a sense of security and belonging. They become a source of identity for children; when a particular rule is always what we do in our family, it becomes as much a ritual as specific holiday celebrations.

Children who understand the reason for family rules are better equipped to obey them when they are away from home. They have a reason for not watching the R-rated horror film, overdosing on television, or participating in some other forbidden activity, even when they may not choose to share that reason with the friend. When a child says, "My parents would kill me!" it is often simply an excuse for avoiding an activity he knows is wrong. It is our role as parents to provide that safety net with clear family rules.

When family rules can stand by themselves, and we have inculcated an internal response that recognizes their importance for the smooth functioning of the family and the well-being of the individual, children are well on their way to becoming moral citizens who are capable of respecting the laws necessary for the optimum functioning and welfare of society.

For Parents

1. Make a list of the rules in your house. If you are a two-parent family, discuss with each other how you would prioritize those rules, what your reasons for the rules are, and what the consequences for failure will be. The older the children, the shorter the list. We cannot hope to hold out for the important things if everything is allowed to become important.
2. Ask your children what the family rules are. You may be surprised to discover what you have taught.
3. Discuss age-appropriate privileges in your house. What is the bedtime for a first-grader, a fifth-grader, etc.? What is the age for double-dating, single-dating? What are the rules about parties? Discussing these things before they become issues can avoid some, but not all, of the arguments.

For Teachers

1. Make a list of the rules in your classroom. Ask the children to consider rules they feel are important.
2. Invite the children to share some important family rules and the reasons behind the rules. Draw parallels for younger children between family rules and laws, such as traffic laws, why both are necessary, and how it hurts when people fail to obey them.

CHAPTER 5

Childhood Rules

Family rules are not the only ones that govern life in childhood. In the neighborhood where you grew up, how many imaginary players could a team have if there were only four real people for the baseball game? Were there special rules to govern their base-running? In hopscotch, could you step in the box after picking up your lucky, or did you have to jump over the empty box until the next turn? How many hot peppers did you have to be able to jump before stepping on the rope if you did not want to be out? Did "Allee, allee in free" signal that you had given up on finding all the people in Hide 'n Seek?

Family rules are set by authority figures. Learning to obey them teaches respect for authority and enables children to begin to comprehend that the needs of the family are often more important than their own particular needs at any given moment. But no matter how carefully we strive to explain to children the need for the rules, and no matter how faithfully we work at inculcating understanding and involvement in the process, many of these rules are intractable and simply must be obeyed, regardless of the child's understanding or feelings on the matter.

Children's games provide another whole world of opportunity for learning how rules function and their importance in

making games work. The rules that govern childhood play sometimes reflect the norms of an adult society, but often have their
own sets of standards that appear unjust or even cruel to adults
who witness them. When my children were growing up, the
youngest child at the bus stop was the last one to get on the bus,
usually insuring that that child had to sit in the most undesir-
able spot. It seemed like a cruel rule, but it dealt effectively with
pushing and shoving and cutting in line, and the children all
respected it because they had decided it themselves.

Most of us can look back on our childhoods and discover
we imposed far more rules on ourselves than the authority figures in our lives ever imposed. Rules for playing games, rules
for nonviolent behavior (no kicking or biting), rules for sharing, even rules for when cheating on homework was not cheating but "helping." All of these rules have as their basis an assumption of equality. Children are willing to give and take directives with those they perceive as "peers." This peer-based rule-
making has several desirable moral outcomes.

In making the rules themselves, children are affirming the
basic necessity of rules for the smooth functioning of any en-
terprise. Although their guidelines may differ greatly from adult
social norms, they still teach the importance of those norms.
Rule-making among peers is probably the closest experience
children will have to the process of law-making in a democratic
society. And rulebreaking among peers has built-in punishment.
Children can be far more cruel than most law enforcement of-
ficers on those who fail to keep the rules. At the very least, a
failure to play by the rules excludes you instantly from the game,
but it can also hold the possibility of excluding you from many
future games. No one wants to hear the reasons why; there is no
court of appeals. If you deserved special consideration because
of age or disability, that would have been decided before the
game began. Once the rules are set, you are expected to abide by
them. And children's rules, unlike adult rules, are always enforced.

Childhood rule-making is the beginning of understanding reciprocity in relationships. You do not abuse your friends; that means no hitting and kicking when you are little, and no lying or revealing secrets as you get older. While parents also have rules about not hitting or lying, and have built-in punishment for violations, parents can be counted on to still be there when the storm has passed. Friends will only take so much before they stop being your friends. Relationship requires honesty, faithfulness, and trust, and childhood is the place for learning these skills. The ability to sustain a healthy peer relationship is one of the indicators of healthy moral development in the child.

If we accept all of this as true, then it is imperative that we look at the over-involvement of young children in organized sports. I am not referring to all the arguments against allowing children whose bones are not fully developed to play football, or permitting children whose sense of balance is still undeveloped to play ice hockey. My concern is with depriving children whose sense of morality is not yet fully developed of the opportunity to play games where they—not adults or rule books—are the principal rulemakers and enforcers, where the rules are based on childhood norms that are often different from adult standards, and where winning and losing, totally divorced from adult expectations, are simply part of playing the game.

Respect for authority does not come only from the consistent, inductive enforcement of reasonable family rules, no matter how important this may be. It is not grounded simply in disciplined and respectful classrooms, despite the tremendous importance of reverent teachers.

Respect for the rules that govern a society also comes from the opportunity to make and enforce those rules for ourselves, and to live with the consequences of our own failures. This is the opportunity of sandlot baseball, jump rope, and hopscotch. This is the legacy of childhood and it should not be dismissed too lightly in favor of T-ball, Pee-Wee Football, and other leagues of watered-down versions of adult games.

For Parents

1. Provide opportunities for your children to play with other children. It may not be safe to do that in your area without careful supervision, but it is always possible to make it structure-free play. Encourage the children to make up games. Teach some from your own childhood if they do not know how to create play for themselves.
2. Play games with your children where they are allowed to set the rules. Once the rules are decided upon, insist that everyone follow them.

For Teachers

1. Create activities, lessons, and games that involve making rules. Give children the opportunity to discover how the rules must be made and to find ways to enforce them.

CHAPTER 6

To Be or Not to Be

Every year our parish held a Christmas country fair. Each of our three children would be given 25 cents to spend, and the manner in which they went about spending it formed an interesting study in the process of decision making. Liz, the youngest, would head straight for the penny auction, put all her money into chances, and place the chances in the cups before the objects she hoped to win. She was convinced she could get more for her quarter in this manner, although she never actually won anything. Jon, the oldest, would walk around the hall quickly, then return to two or three objects. Within the first fifteen minutes, a portion of his quarter would be spent on one of them, and the rest would be reserved for food. The afternoon always ended with Becky, our middle child, becoming frantic as we got ready to leave. She never managed to spend a single penny of her quarter before the end of the day. Each year, we would walk around the hall with her, only to find the things she had originally liked but could not bring herself to buy all been sold. Every year she would struggle as we grew restless, finally settling on something just to be able to say she bought it at the fair. It was Becky who taught us how difficult it is for some children to learn to make decisions.

Decision making is one of the most important life skills to

be acquired in early childhood. For most of us, each day is a series of decisions, from what to wear to what company to invest in. For those who fail to develop comfortable and efficient ways to consider alternatives and make decisions, enormous amounts of time and energy can be wasted on mundane things, while major decisions are put off until a crisis develops. Despite the fact that children from the same family can have very different levels of proficiency in this art, as my own three clearly demonstrated, parenting styles still exercise an enormous influence on the ability of children to make decisions.

Children who come from extremely strict, autocratic households have little opportunity for making decisions. Well-meaning parents, whose basic desire is to support and protect their children, can fall into the trap of making all the decisions and presenting them as rules for good behavior. Rules in these families often imply force as a means of compliance. Even innocuous decisions about clothing and food are made by parents on the basis of what they believe to be appropriate or healthy; decisions about leisure activities, school, church, and other important areas of life are dominated by authority figures with a desperate need for their children to be well-mannered and well-behaved at all times. These children, when faced with the inevitability of making their own decisions, will often become rebellious, choosing "against" whatever has been chosen for them in the past, or procrastinate and delay making any decision until it is made by default.

Children in extremely permissive households are allowed to make all their own decisions, but are often not required to follow through with them. When a decision works out badly, parents intervene to protect the child from the consequences of his actions. These children can grow up to be adults who can make decisions, but may do so selfishly, with little thought given to the effects of their actions on everyone around them. The ultimate test of their decisions is whether or not "it works for me." The ultimate goal of such decisions is self-fulfillment. Not only do these children fail to learn the moral ethic of care for the community, they frequently find it difficult to persevere in decisions whose consequences are unpleasant.

The vast majority of our families fall somewhere between these two extremes, with the children within them covering a spectrum of decision-making abilities. As parents and teachers, we can foster that ability by offering children the opportunity to make decisions whenever we are willing to live with the consequences of their choices. Discussing decisions, making lists of the pros and cons, exploring the effects a decision will have on others, telling stories where the principal characters are called on to make important decisions and weighing the results of their choices, all offer children practice in a very important art. The discussion itself also models the importance of talking through decisions with those whose opinions we respect and trust. Insisting that children follow through on the decisions they have made, and letting them live with the consequences, may seem harsh at times, but it is the only way children learn to take responsibility for their lives.

All important decisions require prayer. Whatever we may personally believe about the role God should play in the decisions in our lives, it is simply obvious that some decisions are spiritually and emotionally more life-giving for ourselves and for the world. We need to teach our children to sit quietly with their decisions, the pros and cons, their fears and their hopes, and open their hearts to the presence of God. This is not a time for talking to God as much as it is a time for listening, listening to God and listening to the Spirit within us, who frequently speaks through our bodies and our emotions. Does the thought of a decision make us tense and edgy, angry, afraid? Can we feel our necks stiffening, our stomachs getting queasy? Does it fill us with a sense of satisfaction, peace, excitement? Does it just feel right? Many of my decisions as a child were made at the top of my favorite tree or lying on the grass watching the clouds. Today's children frequently lack the quiet time and space for

developing the art of discernment. Discussing important decisions with children needs to be followed up with an invitation
to go sit quietly and listen to what God and their own bodies
may have to say on this.

Despite our best efforts, children will develop diverse skills
at this, simply because their personalities are so different. When
it came to college decision making, we had one child who applied to every appealing school, was accepted, and wanted all of
them; one who applied to a few but had already chosen one
even before the results came back; and one whose acceptance
had to be sent by overnight mail. Can you guess who is who?

For Parents

1. On the continuum of autocratic to permissive family structure, where does your family fall? Which decisions do you
   find easiest to share with your children? Which are the hardest?
2. Offer small children the opportunity to make decisions by
   allowing them to choose between two acceptable choices,
   such as two possible outfits for school, two suggestions for
   lunch, etc. Insist they stick to the choice, once it is made.
3. Have family discussions about major family decisions. Be
   honest about which parts of the decision must be made regardless of children's feelings, but consider their input in
   whatever way is possible. Include the decision in your family prayer.
4. Give children freedom (within reason) to make decisions
   for themselves in things that affect their own lives, such as
   decorations for a birthday party, costumes for Halloween,
   projects for science fairs. Allow them to live with the consequences of their mistakes.

For Teachers

1. Explore the lives of saints, such as Maximilian Kolbe, or famous people like Abraham Lincoln, who had to make enormous decisions that affected the lives of others.

2. Help children develop a "code of honor" for weighing decisions. Such a code should include, "How will this decision affect the people who care about me?" "How will my decision help/hurt others?"

PART II

Moral Issues Facing Today's Children

IT WAS JUST TURNING NINE IN THE MORNING when my twenty-four-year-old son arrived in the kitchen, looking ashen and totally panicked.

"I overslept! My alarm didn't go off! If my thesis isn't in the professor's office by 10:00 a.m., he will not accept it! They said no excuses, no faxes, nothing. I'm out!"

Columbia University is at least an hour and a half away, on a good day with no traffic. My son had stopped home the night before, on his way back from visiting his girlfriend at Dartmouth. Exhausted from a weekend spent trying to find a tow truck to get his car out of a snow-covered hole, he had decided to crash at our house and had overslept.

We suggested he call and explain about the car trouble. It was legitimate; he had spent the weekend struggling with it. It was the real reason he had not traveled to New York the night before.

"It's not true. I could have been there this morning. I am not there because the alarm didn't go off and I overslept. I can't lie."

We didn't want him to lie, or did we? There really were extenuating circumstances; he had never been late with anything before. We knew his professor would want to give him a break, but he would need an excuse. Whatever he did, though, he was going to have to do it fast.

He called the university and told the simple truth, he had overslept, with none of the embellishments we had recommended. I suspect the secretary who answered the phone was simply astonished. She instructed him to fax the thesis, and by the time he reached New York, there was an e-mail message from his professor, saying it was accepted and that it looked good.

Children today are faced with a large variety of complex moral dilemmas, many of them capable of stretching our own far more mature moral restraints. Part II of this book looks at some of the issues our children face, from sibling rivalry to family divorce, from cheating to bullying. The list is by no means exhaustive, and the advice is limited to information on the causes of some of the problems. But perhaps a greater appreciation of the struggles our children face daily will offer us some insights into the ways we can support and help.

The message from my son's professor was not the only one waiting for him when he got back to school. There was one of those multi-forwarded e-mails that had arrived the previous Saturday. The story it contained would have been strange to receive on any day, strangest of all on this day.

> Two young men were taking chemistry at Columbia and their exam was Monday. Since they were both carrying A's going into the exam, they decided to visit friends at the University of Connecticut and party over the weekend, then get back in time to study Sunday night. They partied so heavily Saturday night, they slept through Sunday. They rose early Monday and drove back to the city, but decided not to take the exam without the extra study. They approached the professor after the test and explained that they had been in Connecticut and had had a flat tire. Because they had no spare, they had to wait several hours for help, and simply had not been able to make it back in time for the test. The professor agreed to let them take a make-up the following day and the two left congratulating each other on their story.
>
> The next day, the professor gave them each an exam and sent them to different rooms. The first question

was worth five points. It was an easy problem on molecular structure and both sailed through it and turned the page. The second question was worth ninety-five points and asked simply: *"Which tire?"*

Integrity, even in today's world, is a force to be reckoned with.

CHAPTER 7

"Mom Always Loved You Best"

I am the second child in my family. My older sister always got the new coats, the new dresses, the new ice skates, the new bike, and I got her hand-me-downs. I detested her for being bigger and bossier, for getting the front seat of the car, and, most of all, for being first.

My older sister tells a very different story. She complains of earlier curfews and greater responsibilities, countless arguments designed to make my parents more reasonable and make the lives of her three younger siblings far easier than hers had been. My two younger siblings complain that Mom never went to their PTA meetings, after being president of PTA for most of the years both my sister and I were in school. She had given up trying her limited sewing on Halloween costumes long before they reached trick-or-treating age, and she never read *The Christmas Carol* aloud during any Advent within their memories.

Sibling rivalry is as old as humanity. After the pride of Adam and Eve, it is the first source of sin related in the Bible, and continues to play an active role in almost every Scripture story in which a family figures prominently, from Cain and Abel down through Joseph and right up to the Prodigal Son. It fills the pages of today's newspapers with tragic stories, and is capable of making the lives of very ordinary children totally miserable. The dynamic that creates it is almost impossible to alter, but understanding what is happening may enable us to deal more effectively with the problems it creates.

I was the baby in our house for six years, a distinction of honor that was always mentioned when my parents introduced us. The morning my mother told me, in a tone of excitement mixed with awe, that we were going to have a "new baby," I clearly remember thinking, "So what's the matter with the old one?" Sibling rivalry begins with being asked to surrender to a new brother or sister our own place at the center and our exclusive claim on our parents, especially our mothers. It happens before we are old enough to understand the baby's need for this special attention, or wise enough to see that this baby, too, will outgrow this position. All the efforts of parents to include an older child are not capable of overcoming the simple biological reality of infancy.

Losing one's position at the center is never easy, but less painful if a child feels secure in his or her place in the family. Family is the community that first teaches us that there are other important people in the universe besides ourselves. As children, we need enough responsibility to feel essential to the well-being of the family as a whole, and enough "age privileges" to make growing up and moving out of the "center" attractive.

In an automated society where so many tasks are handled by machinery, jobs once understood as belonging to the children have become less essential, leaving them bereft of a sense of responsibility that many of us took for granted, no matter how much we grumbled about it. Laundry is often not hung on lines or even folded, ironing is limited, families who do manage family meals often don't bother setting the table, and dishwashers handle the cleanup. Children's lives have become filled with projects, sports, and lessons that benefit themselves, but these do little or nothing to reinforce their own place in the family.

Age-appropriate tasks help children see themselves as essential. One of the things my own children loved about camping was the importance of the roles they fulfilled: carrying water, finding firewood, replacing the ice. Dusting, vacuuming, watering plants, cooking meals, doing laundry, are all tasks that can be shared by young people and may provide opportunities for parents to single out a child for special attention, while accomplishing a job together. The less "work" we ask our children to do for the family as a whole, the less sense of family they will have. Interdependence may not always be an antidote to rivalry, but it is a less receptive climate for jealousy.

Age-appropriate privileges, such as later bedtimes, having your own alarm clock and being responsible for getting yourself up, having your own bike and caring for it, later curfews, driving a car, or having a pet, make a very clear statement about what it means to grow up in this family. These are not rights, they are privileges. Offering them at some consistent ages clarifies for children the fact that it has little to do with being loved better. It is simply a part of being a member of this family. These privileges help to mark our particular place in the family at a given moment in time. The stronger our sense of belonging, the more secure we feel in our special place in the family, the less need we have to fight for another's.

There will always be personality conflicts and stresses that come from living closely together. Children will continue to argue over who gets the last cookie or sits in the front seat. These arguments are an important part of growing up. They teach conflict resolution skills we all need and too few develop. Knowing our own special place at the family table offers us a secure way to come together and work toward solutions, while acquiring the ability to surrender a bit of ourselves for the good of the whole.

For Parents

1. Make a list of the privileges in your family and the age at which they are allowed, e.g., having a friend overnight, bedtimes, curfews, staying home alone, first watch, first bike, wearing makeup, driving a car, dating, etc. Many of these things may have already become unspoken traditions in your family. Verbalize them so that everyone understands them and can look forward to them.

2. Make a list of duties and the ages at which children will be expected to take responsibility for tasks in the family: setting the table, doing laundry, making the bed, helping with meals. Take time to teach the way you expect the tasks to be completed. In the beginning, it is more time-consuming than simply doing the tasks ourselves, but it is well worth the effort for the sense of responsibility it offers the children and the help it eventually provides for the family.

3. Set aside time to celebrate individual children. This can be one special day a month where that child gets to choose the meals, pick the game or television program, have the last cookie, sit in the front seat, and generally be the center of everyone's attention. All of us need to know we are special and loved.

For Teachers

1. Explore some of the family conflicts from Scripture: Esau and Jacob, Joseph and his brothers, or the Prodigal Son and his brother. Give the children a chance to explain how each sibling is feeling. Ask if they have ever felt that way. Then ask them to explore how the parents are probably feeling. Children who have been given a good foundation in empathy will be able to begin to look at the situations from several perspectives. Ask what could have been done differently that might have prevented the problems.

2. Invite the children to talk about their own places in the family and the advantages and disadvantages that go with that place.

CHAPTER 8

Home Alone

M y parents both worked. Every day, after the school bus
dropped me off, I would walk to a neighbor's house to
retrieve my little brother and head home. There would be a note
on the kitchen table, describing what needed to be done for supper and clearly detailing which duties belonged to me and which
ones to my older sister. I would peel the potatoes, meet my
younger sister's bus, fix her milk and cookies. The two little ones
and I would be ensconced with "The Mickey Mouse Club" by
the time my older sister returned from working on the high
school yearbook or her part-time job. I would have been a latchkey child, if anyone could have found the keys and if we had
ever found it necessary to lock the doors.

Today, somewhere between two and seven million children
are home alone after school. No one knows how large the number actually is because parents are rightfully fearful about letting this information be known. Not only do their "home alone"
children become the prey of burglars and molesters (despite
the fact that today's doors are almost all locked), but single parents who need to work may face the possibility of losing cus-
tody to a former spouse who can provide someone at home at
all times. While working moms may not be as new a phenom-
enon as some would like to think, the problems facing this

generation of latchkey children are decidedly different, particular to them and overwhelming to their families.

Some latchkey children not only survive, they seem to benefit from the experience, the independence, and the sense of responsibility. Others suffer educationally and emotionally, becoming withdrawn, shy, and fearful. Some become so accustomed to being on their own that they are unwilling to accept the authority of discipline. The past fifteen years have produced a plethora of studies that try to determine what makes that difference.

Before examining some of the points made by those studies, it is necessary to set aside our value judgments. Whether or not both parents should work is not the question here. In many situations, parents must choose to leave children home alone if they are going to be able to live in a neighborhood where it is safe to be home alone. Often, there is only one parent and, therefore, one breadwinner. In some professional families, debts incurred through education can only be paid back when both parents work. Whatever the reasons, we need to find ways to support our home-alone children.

Our generation has tried to console itself with the fact that even if we could not give our children large quantities of time, we could give them quality time, and that that was far more important. But children do not need "quality time" as much as they need us all the time. They need stability and security. How we make ourselves present to them when we are physically absent is just as important as how we spend the time we do have together. All time is quality time in a child's life. The latchkey children who appear to do best in that situation are those for whom there is a strong parental presence, even in the parents' absence. There are several ways to maintain that presence.

One is contact. Children need to be in contact with parents or a parental figure. A call from parents at the time children are expected to be home not only lets them know we are thinking about them, it also insures that they have gotten home safely and are where they belong. An "800" service will allow calls home from work and provide needed peace of mind. If parents cannot call, a trusted friend or neighbor can be enlisted. Crisis numbers, and a phone number of a parent or friend who can be reached by a child who just needs to talk, should be listed by the phone. As parents, we need to remember that a forgotten book or assignment may be a real crisis in the life of our child, as important to them as the contract negotiations they have interrupted are to us.

Family rules are another way to maintain contact when we are away. The importance of family rules was discussed earlier, but specific regulations are needed for when parents are not at home. Clear-cut rules, and the consequences for breaking these rules, need to be formulated and practiced intermittently before a child is left alone on a regular basis. These rules will be dependent on circumstance and ages, and will differ from family to family. But all rules need to include strong guidelines on answering the door, messages to be given on the telephone, and people and activities allowed in the home when parents are not present.

A clear list of duties and the consequences of failing to fulfill them insure that the time alone is not spent solely on the phone or in front of the television set. Children who understand the necessity of the entire family working together fare better. While Mom and/or Dad do their jobs, children are needed to help with household chores and to complete their own job of schoolwork.

Follow-up is the crucial hinge on which everything else rests. This is the hardest step for parents returning home fatigued and stressed out. Have the responsibilities been fulfilled, the homework done, the rules kept? A standard debriefing time, perhaps at the end of supper, after everyone has had a little time to unwind, will remind children that they are accountable for their actions. It will also serve as a time to focus on their day and their needs, and will prove far more effective than flying off the handle the moment we walk through the door and are bombarded with questions, problems, and any messes that might have been created in our absence. The magic word in this situation is not "please." It is "wait." "Wait until after supper." "Wait until we have had a chance to relax." "Wait until after my cup of tea." We need to give ourselves time to switch gears; this will make the follow-up process simpler and more effective for everyone. Major infractions of rules should bring immediate punishment, but the handling of total breakdowns in the system needs to be delayed, whenever possible, to a Saturday or Sunday morning when everyone is rested and more willing to be cooperative.

Parents who work outside the home are not always going to be present when things go wrong or when they are most needed. It is essential to develop a strong parental presence that supports and guides our children in our absence. Keeping the lines of communication open is crucial. If we take our children's problems seriously when they are young, even when those problems interfere radically with our jobs, they will be more apt to call us on the more serious issues.

As a mom, I traveled a lot. When on the road, the number where I could be reached was posted where everyone could find it. I have been awakened before dawn in Alaska by a child who forgot the time difference and wanted to say "Hello" before she went to school and describe her outfit for the day. I have been pulled out of a course I was teaching with an urgent message to call home, only to find it was a child seeking permission to go out with a friend and Dad was not around to ask. I have been tracked down all over the country for input on choosing a dorm for the following college year, breaking up with a boyfriend, and selecting courses to take for the next semester. And I have received the calls we all dread, the ones where a real crisis has occurred, and it is time to drop everything and get home. I have discovered we can remain a strong influence in the lives of our children without always being physically present, and I have discovered there are times when our physical presence is an absolute necessity. If our children can count on us to take them seriously and to make their lives a priority in our own, then I think we can count on them when it becomes necessary to leave them home alone.

For Parents

1. Whether you work full-time, or just occasionally need to leave your children, make a list of home-alone rules, asking your children for input and suggestions. Include consequences for breaking the rules, and follow through.
2. Make sure you have a list of crisis numbers by the phone and that your children always know where they can reach you. If you are on the road, a car phone or a beeper may be a wise investment and worth the cost for the peace of mind it will provide.
3. Ask your children their biggest fears about being home alone. Take these fears seriously and find ways to alleviate them.

For Teachers

1. A lesson on the Ten Commandments can offer an opportunity to discuss the rules that God gave us for the time the divine presence would no longer be manifested in the column of fire and the cloud. We would never be truly "alone," but we were being asked to take responsibility for our actions and to live our lives as the people of God without the visible parental presence. Without invading the children's privacy and asking about being home alone, talk about possible guidelines that families today can have for times that parents can't be present.

CHAPTER 9

When Your Best Isn't Good Enough

Maybe it was a fluke. Maybe it was a lack of research. Or maybe it is a sign of the times, but when I started to put this section together, I found very few articles on cheating in school in the major periodicals, and not a single reference in any book less than five years old. Cheating on spouses, cheating on income tax, cheating in sports still seem to be alive and well, but cheating in school is no longer considered a problem. I would like to believe our children are more honest than we were; I suspect the truth is that cheating in school has become so widespread it is no longer considered dishonest.

Teaching the seventh commandment to children once involved some straightforward ideas on cheating: it is a form of stealing, and "Cheaters only hurt themselves." Today's students quickly point out that it can't be stealing if someone gives it to you. Taking a test from a teacher's desk—now that is stealing and qualifies as cheating. But copying someone else's homework, getting or giving a little generous help on the test, finding out from someone who has already taken the test what the questions are, that is considered just plain common sense.

Cheaters don't hurt themselves; they get good grades, while

they destroy the curve for everyone else. They take away someone else's class rank and place in a good college (where they will
sign an honor code promising not to cheat). They fool teachers
into believing that a lesson has been successfully taught, when
most of the class still does not understand. They make their
peers look dumb in the eyes of friends and parents, who inevi-
tably ask, "Well, what did everyone else get?" Worst of all, cheaters get those who refuse to cheat labeled as "geek" and "nerd."
The peer pressure for drinking, drugs, and sex, pales beside the
peer pressure to cheat. It starts sooner, affects all students, and
lasts a lifetime.

How do we arm today's children to face the pressures their
society places on them to cheat? The concept of cheating as
immoral, as sin, as the breaking of a commandment, has little
power to dissuade in a world where cheating is almost expected
and usually condoned by default. Parents, struggling to succeed
in a cutthroat competitive world, often unwittingly reinforce
the idea that if you want to get ahead, you must do well "at all
cost." A narrow interpretation of the separation of Church and
state has led to a futile attempt at valueless education where
teachers can no longer discuss "honesty." But there is simply no
neutral plateau between honesty and dishonesty; you are honest or you are not.

I asked a group of teens who choose not to cheat just what
enables that kind of choice today. A common thread through
all their answers was the presence of a strong self-image. People
who feel good about themselves have no need to convince others they are something they are not. As one seventeen-year-old
explained, "I failed AP Chem. That doesn't make me a bad person, or even a dumb one. It just means I can't do AP Chem. If I
cheated, I might have passed, but I would still know I can't do it.
It would have just kept other people from knowing. And then
they would expect even more of me."

As they talked, it became clear to me that for today's youth,
cheating is not stealing, it is lying. It is pretending you are

something you are not, usually because you are so certain that who you are will be unacceptable. Like all lying, it becomes a trap. Once you begin to lie, it is necessary to lie again and again to preserve the original falsehood. Parents with unreasonable expectations, teachers whose tests are unfair, kids with not enough time to do everything they are required to do, are all partners in creating a youthful society where cheating often seems like the only option.

Enabling honesty in children begins with teaching them to like themselves. Working at overcoming limitations is an excellent goal, as long as the reason for doing so is not that children see those limits as making them unacceptable people. Part of growing up is becoming adept at setting realistic expectations for ourselves and having those expectations respected and supported by the significant adults in our lives. And, painful though it may be, part of growing up is learning to live with failure, to accept the occasional failure as a necessary corollary to stretching our limits.

Parents need to maintain close contact with teachers from the time children first start school. Share your own goals for your child, and the information only you, the parent, can know. Discuss class expectations and any assignments or tests you feel are unreasonable. Be open to the possibility that your child may have misunderstood, may not have let you know when the work was first assigned, or may not have been paying attention. However, teachers also make mistakes, and most welcome your interest and concern when it is not expressed as an attack. Let the teacher know the high priority you place on honesty. Many teachers are afraid to take a stand with a cheating student because that position may not be supported by parents.

We need to help our children honestly assess the effort they give to all their activities, including school, and to help them to plan their time effectively. We need to discuss with them the priority we put on school and our expectations of them, and we need to remember to keep those expectations reasonable. Our interest in learning will do more to foster interest in them than all our expectations. Discuss news issues, topics for papers, class lessons, and assignments. Our children need to know we are interested in them, in how they are learning and changing, not just in the grades someone else is assigning to that learning. Talk openly about failures; evaluate what went wrong and what could be done differently next time. Celebrate the times children tried their best, even when those efforts were not successful. Encourage children to try the things they are not particularly good at doing and to do those things simply for fun, not for success. Help them to understand that when they have enjoyed themselves and have learned something, they are successful, no matter how anyone else evaluates their efforts or accomplishments.

"Cheating makes you feel bad; it's not worth it," one teen pointed out. When our children feel comfortable with themselves, they will become more astute at recognizing those situations that violate their integrity and lead them to compromise who they are. At that moment, they will be able to decide, "It's not worth it."

For Parents

1. Ask your children in what situations they feel most children are apt to cheat. Remain nonjudgmental so they will feel free to share their answers.
2. Ask your children what they think you would do if they failed a test in school. Talk with them about their answers. Let them know clearly what your expectations are and what you are willing to do to help. Let them know how you feel about cheating.

For Teachers

1. Read the parables in Matthew 20:1-16 and Matthew 25:14-30. The lesson is expressed differently in each, but both point out that God expects us to do the best we can with the opportunities we have been given. Talk about that concept with the students. Christians do not measure success the same way our society does.

2. Take time to do at least one affirmation lesson a year with your classes. There are several affirmation experiences in the *F.I.R.E.* program from Liguori Publications, e.g., "Jesus the Affirmer" in *Becoming Community,* Liguori Publications, 1999, pages 69-78, and many youth ministry handbooks contain ideas.

3. Do a lesson on the failures of saints and famous people, and explore the learning that came out of the failures.

CHAPTER 10

Are You Telling the Truth?

R icky was a fifteen-year-old sophomore who hated school. He had learned to use his chronic asthma quite effectively in avoiding the classroom in the elementary grades, but by high school, his mother had caught on. So when Ricky fell off a ladder on Tuesday evening and whined and complained all night about how much his leg hurt, his mother still sent him off to the bus on Wednesday morning. Before she had a chance to leave for work herself, Ricky's school had called. Even though the school nurse was familiar with Ricky's histrionics, she still felt an x-ray was in order. Reluctantly, his mother took him to the local hospital, where he was admitted with a fractured tibia. Years later, his mother was still berating herself for sending her son to school with a broken leg. For all of us who knew him, Ricky became the classic "boy who cried wolf" story that we told to our children.

All of us want to be able to believe our children, those in our families, those in our classes. There are few things as troubling to parents and teachers alike as a child whose word cannot be trusted. How do some children grow to be people of such integrity that they will suffer all kinds of injustice rather than denigrate themselves by lying, while others seem to have no concept at all of the truth?

Lying is a coping skill. Children learn it as they are acquiring some of the other more acceptable coping skills, such as sharing a toy that two people want, following rules in a game, venting anger and frustration in acceptable ways. Psychologists tell us that lying peaks around the age of six, tapers off at seven, resurges again at eight, then diminishes gradually into the teen years, as children learn more effective means of coping. But the disappearance of lying is not inevitable; it depends on the development of the more effective coping skills.

Psychology recognizes three basic types of lying: protective lying to avoid blame, aggressive lying to hurt another, and fantasy lying to enhance one's prestige. As a parent, I would add avoidance lying to the list. It is probably a subcategory of protective lying, but it occupies such an important place in growing up that it deserves its own discussion. Since lying is a coping skill, recognizing the problem (real or imagined) with which the child is trying to deal may offer the opportunity for suggesting more effective ways of coping.

Protective lying occurs when the child feels threatened. If discipline in a home or classroom is too severe, it is better to risk lying and getting caught than to accept punishment. A parent shouting "Who did this?" will most often meet with sullen silence, the effort to lay blame on someone else, or a manufactured story. Recognizing what has gone wrong and suggesting alternative methods of coping can offer children a safety net and the chance to take responsibility for their actions. The more serious the offense, the greater the need for protection and for suggestions on positive ways to handle the problem. If children grow up with a sense of shame and guilt that helps them to acknowledge that a problem is their responsibility, and a sense of self that lets them know they are capable of repairing the damage in some way, they will have developed a more effective management skill than protective lying.

Unrealistic expectations on the part of a teacher or parents can often set the stage for protective lying. Cheating, as we discussed earlier, has become a form of protective lying for many of our children. Children need to know that truth is more important to us than great accomplishments, that everyone feels like lying when caught in a tough situation, and that the truth always takes courage.

Because the line between fantasy and reality is fairly fluid in childhood, fantasy lying is often truth in the mind of the child. Calvin of *Calvin and Hobbes*™ is the classic example of fantasy lying. Children are very good at convincing themselves that what they want to believe is actually true: they are aliens from another planet, they have magical powers, their stuffed animals or dolls are real, a monster invaded the house and broke the vase, etc. Accusing a young child of lying simply causes confusion; truth is not an objective enough reality to be that easily defined in the mind of the four-year-old. When fantasy lying continues beyond the age of six or seven, it turns into false claims of wealth, or fame, or even misfortune, all designed to bring the child or adult attention and esteem. A strong self-image is the greatest defense against fantasy lying. With the young child, the truth needs to be pointed out clearly, without blaming or accusations. With the older child, efforts need to be made to help the child understand that who he or she is as a person is good and that his or her own particular accomplishments are worthy of respect.

Aggressive lying is the easiest for children to recognize as morally indefensible. Hurting another's character or reputation is no different from hurting a person physically. The adults in a child's life need to set a firm example, reacting just as strongly to detraction as they would to physical fighting. Most of us were taught as children that if you had nothing good to say about someone, you should say nothing at all. Establishing this as a firm rule of the house sends a potent message to children about aggressive lying.

Avoidance lies are probably the ones parents hear the most often: "I'm too sick to go to school," "too tired to do the dishes," "too busy with homework to help with the baby." Avoidance lies can sometimes be handled by addressing the true problem: "I know you don't feel like going to school, and it's okay to complain about it, but you are not really sick. You know how to reach me if you really do need me during the day." Avoidance lies can be dangerous because, when they are believed, it becomes easy for avoidance to be learned as a coping skill for all unpleasant situations.

Discipline with children who lie must be consistent and firm, but it is far more effective, whenever possible, to avoid giving children the opportunity to lie than it is to punish them for it after the fact. If you know a child is lying, confront her with the truth rather than asking a question that may produce another lie. More importantly, affirm children for telling the truth, particularly in situations where you know it is difficult. Tell stories of heroes who told the truth in difficult situations, and stories of family members who qualify as heroes for telling the truth.

Honesty, for the most part, is taught indirectly. Teaching children to take responsibility for their mistakes and failures, teaching them respect for themselves and for others, teaching them to confront the unpleasant, and offering skills for coping all help children develop integrity. No amount of teaching, though, is as important as our example. Only if we are honest with our children and ourselves do we have the right to expect them to be honest with us.

For Parents

1. Talk about the importance of being able to trust one another. Share feelings honestly. Children are adept at sensing emotions, and if we lie to them about how we are feeling, it will produce real confusion with our teaching on honesty. Share a time when it was hard for you to tell the truth.
2. Ask your children when they think a person would feel most like lying and what other options they could choose for coping with the problem.

For Teachers

1. Since lying is a coping skill, initiate discussion on better ways to cope with problems specific to your class or to the particular time of year. For example, "When you know you are going to get a warning notice in math, what can you do besides coming home early and getting it out of the mailbox?"
2. Empathy is the foundation of morality. Ask children how they feel when someone tells lies about them, or lies to them about something that has happened. Ask them to consider what might be done to correct the situation. Children need experience in developing coping skills before the situation arises.

CHAPTER 11

Sticks and Stones

He might have been described as gangly. His arms and legs appeared too long and not properly connected. He walked with the peculiar awkwardness of a fourteen-year-old who has not yet grown into his own body parts or deciphered how to make them work together. He was on the second-string basketball team, but he rarely got to play. He was a loner. His teachers barely noticed him; his parents loved him; his peers victimized him. A gentle, passive soul whose classmates' jeers and taunts were often accurate and always cruel, he had never responded to their ridicule with violence. Never, until the Saturday evening he put a bullet through his head.

Bullying. Anyone who has spent any time in a school yard has watched the bully swoop down on a hapless victim. All of us have stood transfixed with horror as perfectly decent young people followed the bully's lead and joined in the tormenting, perhaps fearing that if they failed to do so, they would be the next victims. Every teacher, scout leader, den mother, or catechist can name the outcast in the group, the one who is slightly different in some way, whom the group has decided is unacceptable and whom they make even more different through isolation.

The noted anthropologist René Girard suggests that every

culture is based on violence, or what he calls "unanimity minus one." Girard says that every group chooses a victim, and in this way is able to achieve unity through isolating the one. It is a sad commentary on our society, but it appears to be borne out in daily experience.

Who becomes the victim of bullying? Usually it is the quiet, passive child, often a peace-loving, cooperative student and dependable, caring sibling and friend. Such children do not fight to defend their own rights or even stand up strongly for themselves, simply because, within their frame of reference, winning is not that important. Once the more aggressive "bully" sees what is perceived as "weakness," he or she attacks. While it is the personality of the victim that attracts the attention of the bully, it is usually something external that becomes the first cause for bullying; something in the way a child is dressed, some manner of speech, some physical feature. The victim usually attempts to placate the bully, giving up the offending article of clothing, offering to share lunch money, etc. This invariably leads to more bullying and the invitation to others to join in the attack. Those who admire the aggressiveness of the bully and those who fear becoming victims themselves will all join in.

The insights of the anthropologist can be helpful in addressing the problem of bullying. The primary reason for bullying is the sense of unity that comes out of a common purpose or common "enemy," and the sense of power this unity gives the leader or bully. Separating the bully from his or her most faithful admirers in a variety of work and play situations can sometimes interrupt the dynamic long enough to establish some healthier relationships.

It is important to remember that the bully is often a child who, while feared by peers, is equally disliked by teachers. The natural leadership skills the bully possesses have little chance of being used in adult-supervised situations because adults do not want to work with this child. Providing the bully with opportunities to exercise leadership in healthier ways gives adults a chance to provide some guidance that the bully may be willing to accept.

Offering gentler ways of creating unity with a variety of community-building techniques can sometimes help in an incipient victim/bully situation, but will have little effect where the relationship is longstanding. Direct adult intervention, while absolutely essential when the bullying becomes physical, can often be disastrous. The victim is perceived as the cause of parental wrath or as "teacher's pet," fueling more hatred and exclusion.

Children are capable of incredible cruelty to one another. Those who are gentler by nature need our help in not becoming victims to the bully's need to have a loyal following. As adults, we may abhor the idea of "following the crowd," but children need us to respect their need to "fit in," particularly those children who find it difficult. This does not mean abandoning our standards or forsaking all limits. It does mean listening to the child, compromising on clothes, shoes, backpacks, and other ways children label each other as different. It means making a little extra effort to enable the gentle child to fit in with peers, especially the gentle boy. It also means not pushing children into peer situations they feel unready and unable to handle. Children should always have the option of saying "My parents don't allow it" to anything they are not ready to manage, from school dances to sports.

Jesus asked us to turn the other cheek. The command is to refrain from returning violence for violence, anger for anger, not to lie down and become a doormat. We are to love others as we love ourselves, and it is not loving ourselves when we allow others to walk all over us. It is not truly loving our enemy either, since it is not in any child's best interest to allow him or her to become a bully. Children need to be taught the art of the peaceful but quick rejoinder that can take the wind out of a bully's sails. Forrest Gump's mother taught him well, and Forrest has done us all a favor by giving us the expression, "Stupid is as stupid does." A strong verbal comeback can sometimes be effective with the bully who has not gained any momentum. It communicates clearly, "I don't intend to permit you to hurt me, so you may as well give up before you make yourself look foolish."

Family is the safest place for us to learn how to stand up for ourselves, and children should be encouraged to do so, respectfully but with assertiveness. While the shy, passive child may make a parent's life easy, it is quite possible that child is making his own life hell. Every child is not born to be outgoing and gregarious, but even the quietest child can learn to be assertive. As parents, it is important for us to remember the difference between teaching respect, especially respectful silence, and demanding the kind of submissiveness that is capable of making a child an easy victim. Even though most children need to be taught not to "talk back," the child who never talks back needs to be taught how.

Sticks and stones will break your bones, but it is important for those of us who deal with children to remember that names can also hurt you. Sometimes the wounds are fatal.

For Parents

1. Bullies and victims are a definite minority, but as parents, it is important for us to be aware of either one in the family. Listen carefully to repeated complaints of being "picked on," and check with teachers and scout leaders for the seriousness of the issues. Simple commands to "Stand up for yourself" are not enough to make that possible. While all children eventually experience some problems from bullies, the family of a child who frequently becomes a victim may need some professional help.

2. Read stories about victims and bullies, and discuss situations in which bullying occurs. Offer children ideas on verbal responses and have them try them out at home. Try to help children with a tendency to bully to recognize how that

makes others feel. A child with a strongly developed sense of empathy is less apt to be a bully.

For Teachers

1. Read John 2:13-25. Is Jesus being a bully or responding to those who are bullying the poor? Point out to children that the priests are not afraid of what Jesus has done. He does not scare people. They are afraid of his authority. They are afraid of the fact that he is so sure of himself. How do we become that sure of ourselves?

2. What did Jesus mean when he told us to love our enemies? Hold a class discussion on the loving response for bullying. Use stories of bullying, and invite children to role-play both bully and victim and share how each feels.

CHAPTER 12

To Have and to Hold

Olivia was my best friend in fourth grade. We went to the same public school, where we were staunch rivals in math, captains of choice for the spelling bees, and inseparable on the playground. We were both the second of three daughters; we both had a new little brother that year. We sang together in the children's choir, and we spent countless hours in each other's homes.

To be sure, there were a few differences. Olivia walked to school and I rode the bus. My long, dark hair was always braided neatly, while Olivia's equally long, equally dark hair hung loose. Olivia was docile and tended to be teacher's pet, while I was feisty and tended to be more of a leader. My father was president of the Holy Name society, while Olivia's father was going to hell.

The Franciscans who taught our catechism classes had made that very clear: outside the Church there was no salvation. And Olivia's dad was definitely outside the Church. Today, with our greater command of theological language, we would probably call him an agnostic, but back then, he was a pagan, like the pagan babies we redeemed with our nickels. He had no religion, and Olivia and I worried about him incessantly and prayed for him constantly. We devised "plans" for getting him into heaven with the rest of his family, leaving catechisms on the seat of his truck and rosaries on his pillow. On November 2, we dashed in and out of church, freeing souls from purgatory to intercede for him. (In the pre-Vatican II Church, on All Souls' Day, every separate visit to the Blessed Sacrament in which three Our Fathers, three Hail Marys, and three Glory Bes were said, gained a plenary indulgence for a soul in purgatory. These souls would be forever in your debt.)

Olivia died of a massive coronary when we were twenty-five years old. Her own children grew up in a gentler Church, free from fear for their grandfather's eternal salvation. Rahner had taught us all about "anonymous Christians" and "implicit faith," and the Second Vatican Council had accepted God's freedom to save even those we Catholics believed were unacceptable. We no longer teach hellfire and brimstone, but there is still an unforgivable sin to trouble the hearts of our children.

Thirty to seventy percent of the children in our churches and classrooms will experience a divorce in their families. We have all become painfully aware of the emotional and psychological impact of divorce on children, their anguish in the face of remarriage, and the difficult adjustments inherent in blended families. But what is frequently overlooked is the spiritual impact created by divorce and remarriage on the consciences of children in a Church that still struggles mightily to accept either.

None of the adults in my young life had any idea of the fears they had instilled in me or Olivia. We underestimate the impact of our words, particularly our words about religion, on children. As parents and teachers, it is important that we think through carefully what we teach about marriage so that our lessons become healing for children struggling with the reality of divorce. In teaching about sacraments, we must be aware of the children whose parents no longer feel welcome to celebrate reconciliation and Eucharist, and not teach these sacraments as requirements for being holy people or for living a good life.

In the first four centuries of Christianity, there were sins the Church felt it was unable to forgive, among them, murder and apostasy. It wasn't that the Church believed that God could not forgive these sins. The community continually prayed for forgiveness for the sinner; they simply believed that the holiness of the community would not be maintained if such sinners were welcomed back. Such sins were incompatible with being a Christian. It took the Church several hundred years to realize that such a stance was irreconcilable with the forgiveness of God that Jesus proclaimed.

A similar dilemma faces the Church today. Is it possible for the Church to hold up the ideal of the indissolubility of marriage if it is willing, at the same time, to allow those who have failed to marry again with the Church's blessing? The teaching of Jesus is clear: marriage is forever, and forever is what we all hope for when we enter into marriage. But marriage happens between humans, and human beings fail. We cannot add a concern over the spiritual well-being and salvation of their parents to the fear and guilt many children already feel over the divorce in their families. We cannot present marriage as so sacred that children will grow up, as many of us did, willing to stay with abusive spouses and remain in mutually destructive situations for the sake of "saving the marriage." The covenant of marriage can never be more important than the people who enter into the covenant.

The Church will continue to struggle with the present dilemma. It is for those of us in pastoral practice to reassure children that the Church is still learning and changing, that God's mercy and forgiveness is great enough to encompass all our failures, and that heaven has room for all of us, even Olivia's dad.

For Parents

1. If you have experienced a divorce in your family, ask the children about their biggest fears. Talk about what it means to you spiritually, and how you are resolving that dilemma. Invite them to share with you anything they may be told in religious education classes. Reassure them that you will not be hurt, and would like to be able to help them to handle any misinformation or misunderstanding. Handle the negative situations as calmly as possible, and try not to condemn. It will only further confuse the children.

2. Even if there is no divorce in your family, talk with children about the impact of divorce on families. Many of their friends will have experienced a divorce. Remind them that there are two sides in every problem. Encourage them not to assist their friends in taking sides. This is an opportunity to foster empathy. How do they think each of the people in the family is feeling? Is there anything they can do to help?

3. Talk often with children about the importance of choosing a marriage partner carefully and about waiting until they are old enough to make a mature decision. Discuss some of the reasons for avoiding early sex and the possibility of pregnancy, both of which might precipitate an early marriage.

For Teachers

1. Discuss what kinds of things help and hurt a marriage. Ask children what they want in a spouse, what they would find hard to forgive, and why. Let the children know the Church teaches that marriage is forever, but it is struggling with how to help people when marriages fail.

2. If you are working with older children, explain the Church's dilemma with the problem of divorce and remarriage. Discuss the annulment process. Explain that annulment does not mean that the couple was not legally married; it does not make the children illegitimate. An annulment means

that one of the couple was not able to enter into a sacramental covenant, and therefore, the couple is not truly married in the eyes of the Church. This leaves them free to divorce and remarry. If this is a big issue in your community, invite someone from the marriage tribunal to discuss this process with your class.

3. Discuss with all age groups the things that make a strong marriage. Review the processes taught in the decision-making chapter of this book, and ask students to consider how they would apply these to the decision to marry and to the choice of spouse.

CHAPTER 13

Do You Mind If
I Smoke?

The splashy, appealing ads with sunsets or landscapes and "totally cool" people still capture the back covers of a plethora of magazines, despite the Surgeon General's warning printed unobtrusively at the bottom. Cigarette commercials no longer crowd the airways, but cigarette machines can still be found, along with convenience store owners willing to break the law by selling cigarettes to those under age. While more airports, flights, restaurant chains, and public buildings become smoke-free, supporting the middle-age, middle-class yuppies who seek to kick the habit, smoking continues to rise among the young, especially high school girls, and the age for starting to smoke continues to get younger. Japan has marketed a candy flavored cigarette in an obvious attempt to appeal to the latest stronghold of nicotine addicts. If they succeed in exporting it, we can look forward to an even sharper rise in smoking among an ever younger population.

What has given cigarettes their appeal? Our children are exposed to pictures, and often real samples of lungs destroyed by cigarette smoke, of teeth and fingers disgustingly stained by nicotine. We give statistics on lung cancer and cigarette taxes.

All but the youngest know the physical and financial costs of the habit. Yet they continue to smoke. Are all our efforts simply increasing the appeal to young people who want to show their autonomy by defying authority? With medicine predicting another four hundred thousand deaths this year due to smoking, all of us must do something to confront this problem.

As the smoking age has continued to drop and our recognition of nicotine as an addiction has grown, our educational systems have taken an anti-smoking message once devised for preteens and teens (and often effective with them) and presented it to nine- and ten-year-olds. It is time to rethink this strategy, both in our families and in our classrooms.

Smoking is a moral issue that belongs with any family or class discussion of creation and the wonderful bodies God gave us. Six years of age is not too early to teach a child that anything that brings us physical enjoyment is capable of being abused. While God meant us to find pleasure in eating and drinking, God certainly did not mean for us to eat until we are sick, or drink until we fall down drunk or destroy our livers or our renal systems. We were meant to enjoy our bodies, but we do not have the right to damage them or to use any of our physical powers irresponsibly. As parents, we provide a powerful example when we insist on reasonable diets and exercise and practice both in our own lives, when we limit alcohol, and use both prescription and over-the-counter medications responsibly. The fifth commandment's mandate against suicide applies not just to death but to anything destructive we do to our bodies, including smoking.

Slow suicide by nicotine has been effectively presented to our teens by inviting people whose smoking habit has led to dependence on oxygen tanks for survival to share their story in our homes, classrooms, and youth groups. Despite the fact that teenagers think of themselves as immortal, they do believe in the mortality of others, and are subdued when they confront it. The message has been a powerful, if somewhat temporary, deterrent for teens not already addicted. For most younger children, however, death is simply not part of their reality at all. The few who are able to recognize the signs of impending death will probably fail to make the connection with smoking. And those youngsters who are simply uncomfortable in the presence of such suffering will tend to act in inappropriate ways that can range from rude to cruel.

Sports heroes and famous personalities will have a far greater effect on the hero-worshiping 80s and 90s. Stories of how they conquered the addiction or resisted those who tried to get them to smoke when they were younger are especially appealing and effective at this age. Since young children are not watching the news programs or reading the news magazines that highlight these stories, it is our role as parents to watch for them and make them available to our children. People in your own area whom the children see as "heroes"—from winning coaches to political leaders—would make very convincing guests for catechetical classes that deal with caring for your body as part of the fifth commandment.

The attempt to portray smoking as a disgusting habit that stains your hands and teeth and makes your hair and clothing smell can also be a point of appeal with young teens, but it is a misguided strategy with the eight- to ten-year-olds. After three children of my own and a stint teaching fourth grade, I am convinced nine-year-olds make a career out of being disgusting. This is the year for learning to belch volubly, swear effusively, and make revolting messes out of the food on their dinner plates or in their lunch boxes. This is the year when they can get in the tub, or turn on the shower, and still manage to come out bone-dry and filthy. If smoking disgusts the adults in their lives, that can definitely add to, rather than lessen, its appeal.

However, eight- to ten-year-olds is also the age for "law and order." The fact that more and more states are questioning the "right" of smokers to injure the rest of us with secondary smoke, and are passing laws to prevent this, will spark the interest of

the justice-oriented nine-year-old. Not only are we hurting ourselves when we smoke, there is ample evidence today that we
are hurting everyone around us. For children raised with a sense
of social responsibility and empathy, this can be a powerful
message.

There is no surefire way to prevent children from beginning to smoke without being with them twenty-four hours a
day. But we can be alert to who their friends are, to the amount
of money they have and are spending, and to the smell of cigarette smoke on clothing and hair. If we are aware of a problem
beginning, we need to resist the temptation to brush it aside as
something all kids try at this age. It is true that many of us tried
it and stopped, but it is also true that the cigarettes being sold
today, in spite of advertising to the contrary, are as addictive as
anything we were exposed to as children, and there is far greater
knowledge of the damage they do. Today's parents have an obligation to intervene before a rebellious child becomes an addicted
one.

As parents, there simply are no substitutes for good example
and vigilance. When we allow people to smoke in our homes,
we are granting tacit approval to something we believe is wrong.
We are allowing the smokers to make others ill and to give bad
example to our children. I am aware that this can be especially
difficult when the smokers are beloved relatives, having had a
mother who smoked, but that will only make our "no smoking
in the house" policy an even more powerful lesson.

I remember an incident, long before the use of seat belts
became required by law, when I got into a friend's car and was
asked if I would please buckle up. As I fumbled around the
middle of the front seat looking for the belt, my friend said softly,
"You are far too important to us for us to let you risk hurting
yourself." Perhaps this is the response we all need to learn to
make when someone asks: "Do you mind if I smoke?"

For Parents

1. Check into what your schools are offering as an anti-smoking message. Be aware of the age-appropriateness of the materials. The *American Cancer Society* has videos available, designed to appeal to the new, younger potential smokers. Encourage your school to borrow them.

2. Make "no smoking" a standard policy in your home and explain why to your children. Choose the "No Smoking" sections in restaurants, and let your children know about the effects of secondary smoke.

3. Drug and alcohol abuse are among the more serious problems facing our children. Become aware of the education your schools offer in these areas, and if you suspect a problem, seek professional help immediately. These are issues far too serious for our "home remedies."

For Teachers

1. Include an anti-abuse message as part of any teaching of the fifth commandment. Check with the *American Cancer Society* for videos available. Invite guests to address students: for younger children, those they will see as heroes, for older children, those living with the results of addiction.

2. Become aware of laws being passed to protect nonsmokers from secondary smoke. Discuss these with your students. Have them debate the rights of the smoker versus the rights of the nonsmoker. Remain detached and nonjudgmental in order to give students the opportunity to explore their feelings on the matter.

CHAPTER 14

Why Wait?

If sex is supposed to be such a good thing, and it is supposed to make you feel so close to someone, why should you wait till you are married? How come you say you should only have sex with the person you marry?"

We were gathered around the supper table, just the five of us, and I was grateful it was an evening without company. The question had come from our ten-year-old. Liz has always had a wonderful ability to speak the questions no one else will ask. Her supper table questions have afforded her father and I many opportunities to share our own moral views with our less out-spoken older children. At the same time, they have offered the two of them the chance to argue, question, and challenge our opinions under the guise of "discussing" with their younger sibling.

At this moment, I was painfully aware of the impact of the media on our children. The question would not have occurred to me at age ten; I would not have had the knowledge needed to ask it. The commercials, as well as the stories on television and in the movies, all touted sexual desirability. While we had tried to limit the influence by limiting the media, it still had infil-trated my daughter's life. It had become normal for a child of ten to question if she was sexually desirable, and if this was the case, why shouldn't she act on it? She was not looking for information about sex; we had been teaching that since she was three. She was not interested in the opinion of an outside authority; she already knew what the Church taught. She was looking for a reason that would make sense inside herself.

"Sex is sort of like a good secret," I began, searching for something that would be within her limited experience. "How do you feel when you share a wonderful secret with someone, and that person is the only other person in the world who knows it?" After reflecting on the question for a moment, she decided it made you feel close and special, closer to that person than anyone else in the world.

"What happens when you share that secret with a few other people?" It might still be a wonderful secret, she agreed, but it no longer had the power to make you feel close to each other, to bind you together. And if it was your secret and the other person shared it, you might feel betrayed and angry.

"That's the power of intimacy. It binds us to someone. Sex can do that for us; it can make us feel closer to someone than anyone else in the world. That is its role in marriage. When we have sex with several people, without any real commitment, the sex can still be enjoyable, but it no longer has the power to bind us to another person. And sometimes, if a person we have sex with goes off with someone else, we can end up feeling very angry and betrayed. Like we have given away something the other person really didn't appreciate and respect. Like they betrayed our secret."

It was enough for the moment, but it has come up many times since. As parents, we have to talk to our children frequently and openly about sex. We cannot simply give them rules and hope they will obey them. If we have patterned inductive rule-making all their growing-up years, offering the reasons for the presence of rules in our lives, sex cannot be the one exception, the one subject on which we turn autocratic and offer only the fact that the Church said so. The tremendous growth of sexual activity among our teenagers is ample proof that this approach is not working.

Our children need to be prepared for the passion and desire of early puberty before these overwhelm them. We need to begin talking with them about sex as soon as the first questions arise, letting children know early that this is not a taboo subject. Ten or eleven is not too young to talk with them about the tremendous pressure our society puts on young men to be sexually active, how the concept of "sexual conquests" belittles women and uses them to feed men's egos. They need to be aware that the pressure often leads to young men giving love, or what gets mistaken for love, to get sex. When a loving encounter doesn't lead to sex, those men can wind up feeling angry and cheated.

Young women, on the other hand, are pressured by society to "have someone." Consequently, they may give sex to get love, even though they do not feel the same passion or desire. They expect, by giving themselves fully, they will receive a commitment in return. They can wind up feeling used and betrayed. Young people need to understand the different dynamic that operates between the sexes in these situations. These are the volatile moments that can, at their worst, fuel date rape and teen suicide. At the very least, they can lead to a loss of self esteem or the inability to trust.

As the age for marriage has increased in this country, the age for dating has grown younger, creating a serious dilemma for our youth. Dating is the natural precursor to sex; this is a simple biological reality. By extending the dating period, we are increasing the probability of our teens (and preteens) becoming sexually involved. As parents, we may have limited control over the media, and even less over what our children are reading, but we do have some control over dating. One of the possibilities for helping our children through this difficult time is simply to delay dating. In insisting that our own children wait until they were sixteen, we were hoping they would be better equipped by then to make mature decisions on matters that had the possibility of affecting the rest of their lives. We hoped, by then, that there would have been enough open discussions on sex, on the emotional impact and physical consequences, that the ideas and information would be more readily available to them in a moment of passion.

As well as knowing our moral stand on premarital sex, I think our children have a right to the information they need, before they begin dating, to protect themselves against pregnancy, AIDS, and sexually transmitted diseases. I do not believe that this teaching compromises our own beliefs, if we have shared them clearly for years. I do not think having this information encourages our children to go out and become sexually active, any more than having accident insurance encourages them to drive recklessly. However, I am certain that not having this information can lead to disastrous results.

Twenty-five percent of the people with AIDS in this country are under the age of twenty. Until a few years ago, the teen STD rate and teen pregnancy rate both rose astronomically (the teen pregnancy rate has been dropping in the last couple of years). We would all like our children to choose abstinence, but sex is a powerful passion. If we were not capable of succumbing to it, we would not be human. We need to offer our children tools for protection, then remain nonjudgmental, so that if they do make poor choices, they can approach us for support and love in dealing with the consequences.

Along with creating an atmosphere where sex can be discussed, correct information given, and protection offered, we need to provide our children with good models of loving, committed relationships. If that is not possible, for any reason, within our own marriages, we need to foster friendships with couples able to model that for our children. Strong marriages demonstrate that love is not just about passion and sex; it is also about taking turns getting up with the baby, fighting and making up, and sometimes surrendering our own dream for a time so that we can help to fulfill our spouse's.

The most valuable information we can give to our children is the knowledge that a loving, committed relationship—and all we can do to prepare for it—is well worth the effort and the wait.

For Parents

1. Start discussions on sex early. It will help you to get comfortable with speaking about it with your children. Answer the questions with as much knowledge as you think your child can handle.
2. Check the local library for books you can use in teaching children about their bodies. One you might find helpful: *Sex Is Not a Four-Letter Word! Talking Sex with Children Made Easier* by Patricia F. Miller (Crossroad, 1995).
3. Encourage younger children to ask questions openly in the family. Often, they are not old enough to understand the answers, but the children who are may no longer be willing to ask.

For Teachers

1. Investigate your parish policy on sex education. There is a great deal of controversy over who should teach what, as well as when and how. Check with someone before bringing up any of the issues in class.

CHAPTER 15

Where Have All the Heroes Gone?

When I was five years old, I was certain my grandfather was the most wonderful man in the world. He would sit on our front stoop and tell me stories, whistle softly to the sparrows, who would come and eat from his hand, and sing songs in a brogue that twenty years in this country had failed to diminish. We would walk around our small city block together, stopping as he fixed broken tools and sharpened worn lawn mower blades. He was kind and gentle and caring to every person or animal that crossed our path, and I planned to grow up to be just like him. He was my hero.

Research shows that adults of my generation commonly claim heroes much like mine. In the first five or six years of life, our heroes are those close to us, notable for their presence in our lives, their support, and the love and goodness we experience through them. As we reached our teen years, those whose extraordinary accomplishments attracted our attention, those whose exemplary leadership impacted our world became our heroes. Heroes are seen by most cultures as those who serve principles larger than themselves, who live lives worthy of imitation, and who are catalysts for change. Our heroes were no exception. We built on their inspiration. Scratch the surface of any dedicated, committed, middle-aged adult, and you will find remnants of the heroes of the child.

Heroes are kept alive by their myths, those larger-than-life stories we tell about them; without their myths, heroes die. I am concerned that it is difficult to find a child of seven today who knows the story about George Washington and the cherry tree or Abe Lincoln and the pennies. We have stopped telling the stories because they were not factual. In a coldly scientific society, we have forgotten that the purpose of the myth is not fact-finding, but revealing truths greater than the facts, truths to be imitated, such as the importance of honesty in the lives of two of our truly great leaders.

The shift in the concept of heroes among today's youth is also alarming and deserving of our careful attention. Most teenagers today cite television characters, not real people, as the heroes of their early childhood. Most often singled out for hero status are those characters—"real" or cartoon—whose extraordinary strength or unusual abilities allowed them to achieve good through violence. Parents have surrendered their role as the primary storytellers of their children. Catechists and teachers no longer tell stories of saints and leaders that shape our children's imaginations, create a sense of awe and empathy, and make them want to go and do likewise. Television tells most of the stories to most of the children most of the time.

Once storytelling shifts out of the hands of the primary educators, we give responsibility for fashioning the world of the child to one who does not know the child. Television seldom has the best interests of the child at heart, and often feels no obligation to society at large. Violence is presented as socially acceptable as long as the ends justify the means, and heroic tales have become instruments to sell merchandise in the hands of an electronic media that owes its life to sales.

It is time to reclaim for our children real heroes, people of valor on whose principles they can fashion their own lives. Talk with the children in your classes and your families about the heroes in fiction, heroes in the news, and the ordinary heroes in their neighborhood. Put each hero to the test of the three principles given: people who serve a higher good than themselves, people whose lives are worthy of imitation, and people who are catalysts for change. Many famous people are not heroes; they are simply celebrities who have gained fame and wealth through their talent. Many heroes are not famous; they are simply people who, through dedication and service, have qualified to be called heroic. As parents, we need to reclaim our right to be the primary storyteller and teach our children about the heroes on our own family tree.

Hero worship is a necessary part of maturing. Every culture has its heroes. Let us not allow the cultural consumerism which dominates our media to rob our children of their heritage.

For Parents

1. Create a list of family heroes by telling the stories of the heroic people in your family at supper each night. Keep a list of the heroes on the refrigerator and add to it.
2. Watch the papers and the news for heroes in your neighborhood and in the world. Let children choose a hero they would like to imitate.
3. Make a point of reading and telling stories in the family whenever the opportunity presents itself. In our family, long car rides were a great time for singing together and telling family stories.

For Teachers

1. Saints are heroes who had a spiritual reason for doing what they did. Talk about some of the heroes that are part of our tradition, then invite children to go home and talk with parents about the heroes on their family trees. Have everyone choose a hero to bring back to the class and discuss.

CHAPTER 16

Stressed Out

The year that I started teaching, one of our first graders was rushed to the emergency room with a bleeding ulcer. Days of extensive testing followed to try to determine the cause. It was beyond our comprehension, in the late 1960s, that a six-year-old could have developed an ulcer from stress, but that was the eventual diagnosis. Since then, asthma in children has increased in case numbers and severity, high blood pressure is no longer uncommon in children under fourteen, and child psychiatry has become a flourishing profession. Even small libraries boast a section of books on stress management for children.

A generation of stressed-out baby boomers, anxious to compete and eager to get ahead, has produced a generation of stressed-out children. Parish meetings that once had to be scheduled around parental time constraints now face a far bigger obstacle in children's complex and furiously paced schedules. Attention Deficit Disorder (ADD) has become the most frequently diagnosed learning disability in this country, as we place more and more demands on the attention spans of ever younger children. These children sit in our classes or, more likely, drape themselves over or under our chairs, wriggling, poking, squirming, unable to quiet their bodies, let alone their minds or their spirits.

Webster defines violence as "force accompanied by rapidity." It would also be a good definition of most of our lives. We are a nation in a hurry. We drive at least five or ten miles per hour over the speed limit, whatever the speed limit is; we check for the shortest lines in the supermarket and bank; we expect "instant" everything, from instant dinners for our tables to *Jiffy-Lube*™'s for our cars. We make our business decisions instantly over telephones and send the signed contracts instantly over fax machines or e-mail. We have filled our homes with time-saving devices, but we have filled the time saved even more rapidly. If we are seriously concerned about the violence in our world today, the most important issues may not be gun control and media censorship. The most important issue may be the violence in our own lives of "force accompanied by rapidity."

The lives of many of today's children reflect those of their stressed-out parents. There is little time to "go outside and play," their days have been so filled with organized sports, music lessons, dance, karate, and language lessons, to help them get ahead. High school decisions about what courses to take, what groups to join, what sports to play, have become dominated, for many, by the question of what looks good on college applications. Today's children rarely have the opportunity to relax, play make-believe, or just spend time dreaming. When I try to point this out to parents, I am often told, "But my children just love being so involved." I don't doubt it. But our children may also love candy, and none of us would consider letting a child eat it to the point of getting sick. Today's children are getting sick on the rush, and are in need of a healthy dose of boredom.

Jesus said to his disciples, "Come away to a deserted place all by yourselves and rest a while" (Mark 6:31). They had been busy traveling and teaching, they were tired and "stressed out," and Jesus offered quiet rest in an out-of-the-way place. In a noisy, stressful world, finding a place of external quiet can be the first step in achieving internal peace. Where do the children in your family or your class go when they need to be alone, when they want time to think, or just need to calm down? Do our children even know what it is to take time out to be alone and think quietly? Do they have any idea what to do with time that has not been organized, scheduled, and filled?

My special spot, as a child, was the top of a tall oak tree in our back yard. The tree could only be accessed by climbing on top of a makeshift wooden ladder until you could reach the lowest branch, swinging your feet up around the branch and then pulling the rest of your body up and over. Before I would pull myself up, I would always take care to kick the ladder into the nearby bushes where it was safely out of sight. No one in my house would have dared to climb the tree after me anyway, but I did not want the ladder giving away my whereabouts. Close to the top of my tree, the trunk divided into three branches, forming a comfortable nook for sitting, and the entire neighborhood was visible from this perch. I could manage the climb with an apple in my pocket and a book tucked in my belt, and I would hide away serenely until I was ready to face the world again.

If children do not have a special spot, we need to help them find one. Attics, tree houses, and treetops can all provide quiet spots. If a space can't be found, it can be created in the corner of a bedroom with a few cushions and a special lamp, and a family understanding that people in the special spot are not to be disturbed. Learning how to seek quiet outside themselves helps children to find quiet inside themselves. Unfortunately, in our society, "quiet room" and "quiet corner" have become places of punishment; being required to be quiet has become the common punishment for misdemeanors. "Time out" may be a good name for a punishment that excludes a child from a group; "quiet time" is not. Quiet time needs to be seen as a reward, a chance to curl up and read a favorite book, draw or paint a picture, color, crochet, wood carve, knit. As parents, we need to be the ones to suggest it to the child who has become stressed out studying or practicing, or just overburdened by a full schedule's demands. "Why don't you take some quiet time?"

Quiet is more than the absence of noise; finding a quiet spot also involves finding the time for solitude. Teaching children to take the time needed to "de-stress" requires the same patient, consistent reinforcement as teaching them to take showers, brush their hair, and take care of their clothes, and the learning may prove far more important to their physical well-being.

When Jesus invited us to set our hearts first on the kingdom of God, and everything else would be given to us (Matthew 6:33), he was pointing out a well-known tool in stress management: ordering priorities. It is one of our roles as parents to teach children moderation, not just in eating, but in doing. Look at all the activities that have taken large chunks of your life and of the lives of your children. Which ones are relaxing and fulfilling, and which ones simply add too many demands, expectations, time commitments, and stress to the life of the family? Cut back on stress-producing activities the same way you would cut back on fats in the diet of a child with a tendency to be overweight, or sweets in the diet of a child with poor teeth.

Offering more space and time in the life of a child will not heal the ravages of stress if that time is filled with television. Stress occurs whenever we feel inadequate in handling the problems and situations that confront us. Television continually presents images, conflicts, and violent situations that are far beyond the comprehension of the child watching. As adults, we have become anesthetized to the constant barrage of violence and the normalization of deviant behavior that is so much a part of prime time. It is easy to be unaware of the stress it creates in the mind of a child who still has difficulty distinguishing between the real and the imaginary. There is enough real violence in the streets, and enough real conflict in the homes and families of our children today, without adding another imaginary layer with which they must cope.

Stress is a normal part of life; learning to cope with it is one of the tasks of growing up. But too much stress is unhealthy for any of us, and too much too soon can interfere with maturing.

As parents, we have both the opportunity and the responsibility to limit the stress in our children's lives. We may find that we have become "saviors" by our simple insistence to "Come apart and rest awhile."

For Parents

1. Help your children discover quiet spots, and teach them to use them.
2. When children complain of boredom, don't rush to fill the time with worthwhile activities. Give them time to learn to amuse themselves, to create their own games, and to just sit quietly. Boredom is the time we all need in between thinking projects. We are raising a generation that no longer knows what it means.
3. List all the activities that take up the time in your lives.

For Teachers

1. Take time during class to invite children to journey to their own quiet places in their imaginations. Ask them to listen to the sounds, feel the feelings, and recreate the spot and the quiet in their minds.

CHAPTER 17

Praying by Heart

~

A s a young child, I went to public school. My formal religious education, or catechism class, as we called it, happened in my little country parish after the nine o'clock Mass on
Sunday morning and after school on Monday afternoon. There
was a class for those who had not yet started school, the "prayer
class." The little ones did not have to come on Mondays, but
they were there the rest of the time, and spent most of their
classes reciting memorized prayers. The sacrament classes were
taught by Sisters, the other classes by mothers, and when my
older sister entered eighth grade in a Catholic school in the city,
she was promptly enlisted to teach the prayer class. After all, it
wasn't a very important class. Anyone could teach children to
pray. All you had to do was to review the words, over and over
and over....

Growing up, memorized prayer was the only form of prayer
I learned. No one thought it necessary to explain the words.
They were simply meant to be learned "by heart." In my own
mind, they became linked to superstition and magic. We spent
All Souls' Day dashing in and out of church, saying three Our
Fathers, Hail Marys and Glory Bes, freeing souls from purga-
tory. Thirteen *Memorares* guaranteed an answer to any prayer,
and twelve Glory Be's said daily for twelve days, kneeling before

a statue of the Infant of Prague, hands cupped to receive the blessings that would be poured out, were the answer to every serious need. Some of the lesser needs could be met by "Dear Saint Anthony, lost and found" who would be sure to "send the book around."

But when my own child, not quite three years of age, asked me to substitute the "other Mary prayer" for the Hail Mary during our nightly prayers, I had no idea what he meant. He bowed his head obligingly, joined his hands, and said reverently, "Mary had a little lamb...." I was horrified. I realized that my son thought everything that was memorized was prayer. I decided then that rote prayer was a mistake. It should be saved for those times in church when we all needed to pray in the same words. Children should be taught to pray in their own words, in order to learn that prayer is a conversation with someone you love. While our family spirituality was rich in spontaneous prayer and ritual, rote prayer disappeared from our family vocabulary. Nine years ago, my son, by then twenty-three, was on his way to work when an elderly man with Alzheimer's stepped in front of his car and was killed. There was no alcohol or speeding involved, and in a large city, the entire matter would have been settled in civil court. But this was a small town, and small town justice can be cruel. My son, who had never actually struck anyone in his whole life, now had to deal not only with his own grief over this man's death, but with criminal charges and a possible jail sentence.

We spent months paralyzed by fear and sick with grief. I would doze off at night, only to be awakened by fear, clutching at my stomach and sending me racing to the bathroom to be ill. It became impossible to pray. In the long hours of darkness, I returned to the rote prayers of my childhood, reciting prayers I had forgotten I knew: prayers to Michael the Archangel, prayers against evil, and countless *Memorares*. When my son told me he could no longer pray, I shared what I was doing. He looked at me sadly and said, "You never taught me those prayers."

Rote prayer is not just for the times we need to say the same words. Rote prayer is for the times we have no words. It does not matter if we do not understand the words when we first learn them; we will grow into understanding, and the words will be there when we need them. It is part of our role as catechists and parents to give words to prayer to fill the voids that will come later.

If we want to raise moral children, we must begin by realizing we cannot do it by ourselves. We need to look for support and teach them to ask for support. If we want our children to make moral choices, we must equip them with the resources they will need to live with those choices. It takes courage to tell the truth, to take responsibility for our own actions, to hold on to an unpopular belief or abide by a different standard of conduct. While a strong sense of self and a supportive family backing provide a child with much of the moral fortitude needed to live a life of integrity, there are times when what we can give as parents is simply not enough. We need to teach our children to pray.

While young children may not have a great need for rote prayers in their lives, childhood is still the best time for learning them. They will become the "default setting on their spiritual computers," the command that takes over when no other is given. Then no young adult will be forced into a dark night without words to give voice to his grief and his plea.

For Parents

1. Choose a different rote prayer to teach your child each year. Angel prayers, for bedtime, for morning, for protection, are wonderful prayers for little ones. One line prayers from the psalms, such as "Keep me, O God, as the apple of your eye; protect me in the shadow of your wings," can be taught easily in middle school years, and junior high is an excellent time for learning the Prayer of Saint Francis and the Breastplate of Saint Patrick. My *Family Prayer for Family Times*[4] provides most of the traditional prayers, with guidelines for teaching children to pray.

For Teachers

1. Each year, teach one traditional prayer. Recite it at least once during every class so that children will have committed it to memory.
2. Invite children to make a prayer book of traditional prayers by having them ask older family members what prayers they learned "by heart" as children.

---

[4] Kathleen O'Connell Chesto, *Family Prayers for Family Times—Traditions, Celebrations, and Rituals,* Twenty-Third Publications, 1995.

Conclusion

The instructions for the national essay contest asked the students to consider a serious problem currently facing our world and to describe, not how to solve the problem, but how the world would look when that problem had been overcome. The basic premise was that we needed a vision of where we wanted to go if we ever hoped to get there. A $10,000 college scholarship would be given to the high school junior who created the most outstanding vision for a new world.

Liz struggled for days with her English teacher's invitation to participate in the contest. What did she know about the problems of the world? What kind of a vision could she possibly have at sixteen, and what could she really do about it? To help her get started, I asked her what she considered the most basic problem in our world today, the one on which all others hinged. Her answer startled me: "The loss of childhood."

Childhood, according to my sixteen-year-old, was all about dreaming, imagining what you wanted to be and letting your dreams shape the becoming. For Liz, her own vision of a new world was simply not as important as creating a world in which every child could dream, in which every child would have a vision, because the world would only be changed one dream at a time.

Liz's essay did not win a prize. The profound simplicity of her words may not have impressed the judges, but they remain a challenge to any parent willing to hear. Perhaps it is time to listen to what our children are asking us to give them.

My Vision

A Letter to My Unborn Children[5]

Although you do not yet exist, you are but a hope in the recesses of my mind, I want to give you a vision for the world you will inherit. I hope to hand on a world in which you are free to play and to grow, a world with clean air for flying kites, with green hills for rolling down, sparkling oceans for exploring and snowy beaches for sand castles. I want to give you a room so clean and so tidy that you will want to keep it that way. And I will teach you to care for this room, and I will love you.

I want to give you a world where childhood is valued as an important time for climbing trees, swinging on swings, jumping rope, and most of all, a time for dreaming. Instead of video games, I want to offer you a back yard that holds within it all that your imaginations can create. Instead of uniformed sports, I will give you sandlot baseball, hide-and-seek, red light/green light, and the opportunity to create new games and make new rules that make the games work. With other children, you will be free to make haunted houses and blanket forts, to dress up in old clothes and put on plays for the tea-sipping adults who will have time and who will appreciate you. And I will play with you, and I will love you.

---

[5] Copyright: 1993, Elizabeth Chesto. Used with permission.

I will give you a life filled with stories, the stories we tell and the stories we read together at night. The sounds of the words will be free to make beautiful pictures in your mind, in a world grown tired of suffocating its children with violent images and numbing repetitions. I will give you saints and heroes to emulate, fables to digest, and ballads to sing, so that you will fall in love with the wonder and the goodness that dwell within. And I will share your newfound wonder, and I will love you.

I will give you the opportunity to do tasks within your ability, to learn early in life that there is as much joy in the process of doing a job well as there is in the product of a job well done. We'll do chores that offer their own pleasures, raking leaves to jump in, baking cookies to eat, and waxing floors to slide on. I will never be afraid to seek your help, even as I offer you mine. And I will work with you, and I will love you.

I will give you a garden, even if we have to keep it in a window box, so you can understand the importance of nurturing life in every form. I will give you adults who will listen to you and respect your dreams, so you will have faith in your visions. I will trust you, and you will find in that trust the ability to trust yourself. And I will listen, and I will love you.

Together, we will explore a finger-painted world, where it is OK to mix the colors and to crayon outside the lines. In this many-colored world, we will learn that technology has only answered "how," progress has only answered "when." Art will set free the child within who asks "why," and part of the answer the world so desperately seeks will be the question.

And I will treasure every "why,"
Every painting,
Every puppet show,

Every waxed floor and brushed tooth,
Every sand castle,
Every story,
And every dream,
And always, always, I will love you.

                                           Mommy